Date Due

F

Does Big Business Rule America?

Eugene Bardach
Royall Brandis
Ithiel de Sola Pool
James Q. Wilson
Paul J. Halpern
Clarence J. Brown
David Stockman

Does Big Business Rule America?

Edited by
Robert Hessen

Critical Commentaries on
Charles E. Lindblom's
'Politics and Markets'

Ethics and Public Policy Center
Washington, D.C.

Library of Congress Cataloging in Publication Data
Main entry under title:
Does big business rule America?
  1. Lindblom, Charles Edward, 1917-   . Politics and
markets.   2. Big business—Addresses, essays, lectures.
3. Liberty—Addresses, essays, lectures.   4. Industry—
Social aspects—Addresses, essays, lectures.   5. Com-
parative economics—Addresses, essays, lectures.
I. Hessen, Robert, 1936-   . II. Bardach, Eugene.
III. Ethics and Public Policy Center (Washington, D.C.)
HD82.L4753D6   330   81-9821
ISBN 0-89633-048-6   AACR2

$3.00

Contents

A Historical Note

SOME BOOKS HAVE a longer gestation than others. The present volume was conceived more than three years ago, when the Ethics and Public Policy Center launched its Business and Society project. Paul J. Halpern, then on the Center staff, sensed the significance of Professor Lindblom's newly published *Politics and Markets* and suggested a symposium on it. Many months, manuscripts, and critical reviews later we finally have a slim but pithy volume that will be of interest both to students of political philosophy and to students of economics.

I take this opportunity to thank Dr. Halpern for his prescience and for his work on the early stages of the book and a score of other scholars for their involvement. Special thanks is due Dr. Robert Hessen, a senior research fellow of the Hoover Institution on War, Revolution, and Peace at Stanford University, who pulled the volume together and wrote the illuminating introduction. Dr. Hessen is the author of *In Defense of the Corporation*. The symposium was edited by Carol Friedley Griffith of our Center staff.

ERNEST W. LEFEVER, *President*
Ethics and Public Policy Center

Introduction

BIG BUSINESS DOMINATES American culture and politics and prevents the introduction of central planning in place of a market-oriented economy. This is the thesis of an influential book, *Politics and Markets*,* by Charles E. Lindblom, professor of economics and political science at Yale University.

The book appeared with glowing recommendations from three prominent scholars. Everett C. Ladd, Jr., called it "a great book, certain to be one of the most influential written by a political scientist in the last quarter century." Neil J. Smelser said it was "an extremely important work of exceptional quality and force." And Richard Nelson described it as "new and stunning . . . a powerful and important book that is going to influence the thinking of a lot of people." It was awarded a prize by the American Political Science Association, and its influence has been growing. Its subsequent appearance in paperback virtually ensures that it will be read by thousands of college students during the next decade or two.

Professor Lindblom's method of argument is distinctive. For example, he asserts that corporate executives are really government functionaries. How does he reach this conclusion? He asks us to "imagine a politico-economic system without money and markets"; in such a system, all economic decisions would have to be made by government officials. He does not discuss the feasibility of his imaginary system, nor whether a social system that outlaws

---

Politics and Markets: The World's Political-Economic Systems, New York: Basic Books, 1977; paperback edition by Basic Books and Harper Colophon Books.

1

individual liberty, private property, and free trade is just. Instead he writes:

> In any private enterprise system, a large category of major decisions is *turned over* to businessmen, both small and larger. They are *taken off* the agenda of government. Businessmen thus become a kind of public official and exercise what, on a broad view of their role, are public functions [*Politics and Markets,* p. 172; italics added].

By a similar logic one could argue that parents are government officials too. Why? Because we can imagine a system in which married couples are required to obtain governmental permission before they bear children. But our system does not require this; therefore, in our system, decisions about child-bearing have been "taken off the agenda of government," and those who do make these decisions—prospective parents—are "a kind of public official."

Lindblom arbitrarily creates a society in which all activities and decisions are "public," that is, subject to the political process. By doing so, he transforms freedom and private decisions into aberrations that need to be justified. He does so because private property and economic liberty are the barriers to his political ideal: central planning, a system in which the government dictates how a country's economic resources are to be used.

To Lindblom, the virtues of central planning are self-evident. He offers no explanation of precisely how central planning works or why it is superior to a market-oriented economy—that is, one based on private property, freedom of contract, profit-making, and the right of individuals to choose their jobs. He believes that central planning reflects confidence in human reason, that "it derives from a buoyant or optimistic view of man's intellectual capacities" (p. 248) and from the conviction that "some people in the society are wise and informed enough to ameliorate its problems and guide social change with a high degree of success" (p. 249).

Far from being a champion of reason, however, Lindblom really is advocating intolerance and the suppression of dissenting viewpoints. As Professor James Buchanan has noted:

Somehow, Lindblom seems under the delusion that the idealized notion of a single mind (of an individual or a ruling elite), coordinating everything in society, elevates and honors the intellect of man more than the notion of mutual and spontaneous adjustment among men, each of whom utilizes the information available to him. But where does he leave those whose actions are to be coordinated by the imaginary mastermind? What implicit respect is given to the intelligence of those who are to be the putty to the master's modeling? Where is there room for individual preferences? He gives no answer to these questions and apparently does not even consider them [*Journal of Economic Issues*, March 1979, p. 217].

Lindblom believes that the suppression of individual liberty and economic freedom is unobjectionable if the political processes in a country are democratic. Although he prefers a democratic system to a dictatorship, he does not notice that the difference is bogus if all decisions are to be made in the political arena. If private spheres of action and opportunity are to be outlawed, it scarcely matters whether the dictator is one man—a Lenin or a Mao Tse-tung, for example—or a majority of the voters. The results are identical: individuals are not free to pursue their own interests, to engage in peaceful cooperation and exchange with one another, or to reap the benefits of their own ingenuity and industriousness.

Instead of offering some justification for advocating tyranny by the majority, Lindblom tries to explain why no democratic society has ever adopted central planning and, conversely, why all democratic societies in history have been market-oriented. (In place of the word "democracy" Lindblom uses "polyarchy," which he defines as "rule by many"; it is a term that he and Robert A. Dahl introduced in their 1953 book *Politics, Economics and Welfare*.)

To show that central planning can co-exist with democratic political processes, Lindblom attempts to prove that there is no necessary connection between capitalism and democracy. His method is to pose a rhetorical question: "Can we conceive of a polyarchy [i.e., a democracy] arranged to achieve popular control over a government bent on collective purposes, one much less committed to the traditional individualistic liberties?" (p. 165). In other words, can we conceive of a democratic system that outlaws the free market? His answer, in its entirety, is: "Yes, it is not difficult. Logically, therefore, polyarchy and market are independent. This is an important conclusion." But it isn't a conclusion at all. A conclusion is the end-product of a chain of reasoning, the verdict reached after a painstaking examination of facts, evidence, arguments, and counterarguments. Lindblom's "conclusion" is simply another of his arbitrary assumptions; he asserts as axioms the very points that most need analysis and validation.

He then poses another question: Why haven't any democratic societies "tried to plan production centrally in peacetime"?

> [Do] polyarchal citizens and their leaders simply know, for all the superficial appeal of central planning, that it is in fact not a better solution to their problems than the market system? *They could not possibly know that to be true. No one knows it to be true—or false. It is a matter of dispute.* One would think that at least one polyarchy would experiment, even if for the worst of reasons. But they do not dispute, let alone experiment. It is a deeply puzzling phenomenon [p. 168; italics added].

What is really puzzling is why Lindblom would think that the citizens in a democracy might decide to experiment with central planning, when they can see how it has worked in Soviet Russia under Lenin and Stalin, in China under Mao Tse-tung, and in Cuba under Castro. The results of these experiments were singularly uninspiring, even if one ignores the high costs—terror, repression, tyranny—of obtaining them.

Instead of offering reasons why democracies should choose to experiment with central planning, Lindblom assumes that they would if they could and shifts to the question of who *prevents* them from doing so. His answer is that the experiment is thwarted by those who benefit from the preservation of the status quo: wealthy businessmen and large corporations. They feel threatened by central planning because it will interfere with their existing rights— "rights to control enterprises, rights to organize and dispose of productive assets, and rights to income from them" (p. 168). Central planning, Lindblom notes, "is subversive of . . . the prerogatives, privileges and rights of the business and property-owning groups."

What proof does he offer that these groups have blocked exper-
imentation with central planning? He states:

> Only if the wealthy (or persons allied with them) exercise at all
> times in all polyarchies an extraordinarily disproportionate in-
> fluence on government policy can the challenge of central plan-
> ning to the privileges of property explain the remarkable uni-
> formity of polyarchal hostility to central planning. If we can find
> no other explanation for the hostility, that in itself suggests that
> perhaps they do exercise such an influence [p. 168].

In other words, if democracies fail to experiment with central
planning, it must be because they are dominated by the wealthy.

Is this form of argument plausible? We can test it by substituting
for central planning some other social experiments that have not
been tried anywhere. For example, although Esperanto is simpler
and easier to learn than any existing language, no nation has
adopted it. Would Lindblom view this as evidence that a verbal
elite with a vested interest in the existing languages is exercising
disproportionate powers in all societies? Similarly, no democratic
society has abolished freedom of religious observance. Would
Lindblom therefore conclude that religious leaders have a
stranglehold on all democratic societies?

Before concluding that only the dominance of a wealthy minority or big business prevents democracies from adopting central
planning, Lindblom must show that the majority shares his dislike
of the market system. But he offers no such evidence. He concedes
the absence of widespread antagonism to capitalism—but inter-
prets it as proof that the majority has been brainwashed or indoctrinated!

Lindblom's distinctive method of analysis includes the use of
arbitrary assumptions that defy common sense and the refusal to
allow any facts to contradict his conclusions. These points are well
documented in the essays and reviews collected in this volume.

In the first response in Part One, Eugene Bardach, associate
professor in the Graduate School of Public Policy at the University
of California, Berkeley, argues that Lindblom's thesis is based on
weak evidence and disingenuous theories. Bardach's review was
originally published in *Commentary*.

Royall Brandis, professor of economics at the University of Illinois, Urbana-Champaign, says Lindblom grossly overstates corporate influence and "mind-control" in American life. His review originally appeared in the *Southern Economic Journal*.

Ithiel de Sola Pool, professor of political science at Massachusetts Institute of Technology, argues in a new essay that Lindblom's thesis is untenable because it wrongly equates the general business community with a small group of top executives in major corporations.

James Q. Wilson, a professor of government at Harvard, says Lindblom's thesis is wrong because a disproportionate possession of resources by big business does not necessarily lead to a disproportionate exercise of political power. His review was originally published in the *Wall Street Journal*.

Paul J. Halpern, a political scientist educated at Harvard who has taught at UCLA and American University, challenges Lindblom's thesis by offering alternative explanations of why regulatory laws are not always so strictly enforced as their sponsors originally intended them to be.

Clarence J. Brown is a congressman from Ohio and the ranking Republican on the Joint Economic Committee. Although his article from the *Wall Street Journal* does not mention Lindblom, it is included here because it presents compelling evidence against the claim that big business can dictate its list of demands to a subservient federal government.

Part Two of this volume is a rebuttal by David Stockman of Lindblom's claim that natural resources will be depleted in an economy based on production-for-profit. The claim is invalid, Stockman argues, because it fails to take into account the likelihood of future discoveries of resources based on explorations that are not economically justifiable at the present time. Stockman wrote this essay while he was serving as a member of Congress; subsequently he has become nationally renowned as director of the Office of Management and Budget in the Reagan administration.

The contributors to this volume do not agree with one another in every respect, but we certainly would agree that ideas are weapons in the battle to preserve political and economic freedom in the Western world. These rebuttals to Charles E. Lindblom are intended to provide intellectual ammunition for that effort.

ROBERT HESSEN
Senior Research Fellow
Hoover Institution

June 1981

PART ONE

Pluralism Reconsidered

EUGENE BARDACH

FOR MANY YEARS Charles E. Lindblom, Sterling Professor of Economics and Political Science at Yale, has advocated the political virtues of liberal democracy, the economic virtues of private markets, and the problem-solving virtues of American pluralist politics; but in *Politics and Markets* Lindblom writes as a man whose hopes have been betrayed. "Grossly defective" is the final judgment he passes on "classical liberal and pluralist thought." Since Lindblom has contributed to this body of ideas and interpretations at least as much as any other contemporary American political scientist or economist, this frank reconsideration of his own previous commitments is an occasion for interest—if not, indeed, dismay.

Lindblom's fundamental moral premise seems to be that in the realm of economics there are no "rights," only "privileges." Early in the book he muses on the possible validity of Proudhon's aphorism that "property is theft." By the middle of the book we are told that decisions concerning plant location and "the quality of goods and services" are really "public-policy decisions" that happen to have been "delegated" to businessmen rather than to government officials. Businessmen, and the rest of us as well, may think that such decisions follow property rights, but Lindblom admonishes us that they are artifacts of businessmen's "privileged role in government . . . un-

EUGENE BARDACH is an associate professor in the Graduate School of Public Policy at the University of California, Berkeley. This article is reprinted by permission from the August 1978 issue of "Commentary" magazine; all rights reserved.

matched by any leadership group other than government officials themselves." By the end of the book, even these traditional "privileges" are called into question by emerging "collective purposes" like the search for peace, energy conservation, environmental protection, and economic stability. Lindblom's conclusion: a "restructuring" is needed that "goes to fundamentals of the politico-economic order."

But how to proceed and how far to go? If we will but open our eyes, lessons abound: the Communist societies, says Lindblom, have achieved more equality than Western societies, and they might conceivably be proceeding toward eventual greater freedom as well. The truth of the matter is hard for us to discern, however, partly because Communist achievements have been associated historically with the cruelest and most extensive forms of repression, but partly too, Lindblom alleges, because we have all been indoctrinated by business and corporate interests.

Politics and Markets is evidently designed as a work of counter-propaganda, attempting to undo the effects of alleged corporate and class indoctrination by making markets and "polyarchy" (Lindblom's word for our form of government) look less benign while making bureaucratic central planning and authoritarian government look less terrible. The book aspires to a place in the tradition of political philosophy that begins with Plato and Aristotle and, for Lindblom, culminates in Adam Smith and Karl Marx. This tradition makes use not only of formal analytical and critical methods, like the explication of meanings and the ordering of social data, but also of the indirect methods of rhetoric and persuasion.

And in fact Lindblom's persuasive technique is varied and skillful. For instance, there is an elaborate and studied even-handedness: "In unobscured view, no society looks defensible," he writes. In the U.S.S.R. there are fraudulent trials on false charges, censorship, thought control, and constant intimidation, whereas in the United States "great wealth still leaves a segment of the population in a demoralizing welfare system." There is a reminder of his own fallibility: "I am not pretending impartiality" on the relative flaws in the United States and the U.S.S.R. There is the announced anticipation of being misunderstood: he says he is constrained to "put the point in its most cautious and acceptable form" that "the positive Communist claim to a humanitarian concern for freedom" may in some sense be meaningful and legitimate.

Lindblom's rhetorical skills are not at all contrived. Their effectiveness comes partly from his long record of academic and intellectual accomplishments, and in even greater part from his obvious sincerity. But sincerity is no substitute for wise judgment when it comes to either moral or analytical issues, and, again and again, Lindblom's judgment proves the very reverse of wise.

Is America 'Indefensible'?

Is it really possible, for instance, to accept his judgment that the United States is truly not a defensible society? That it is no more defensible than the Soviet Union? Welfare recipients in the South Bronx may have to make do on a meager stipend and live in slum housing, but the inmates of the Gulag live on considerably less and may neither complain about their condition nor move out. In the United States some businessmen do, as Lindblom asserts, sometimes attempt to control elected officials through campaign contributions or even bribes. In the Soviet Union, of course, such attempts by the unofficial political elite, the Communist party, to control officialdom are unnecessary, because the party has expropriated official power lock, stock, and barrel. If environmental degradation in the United States makes this country "indefensible," the Soviet Union is surely less defensible, though Lindblom fails to say so. As we know from the excellent research of Marshall Goldman, the Soviet record on environmental matters is quite poor; we do not know just how poor since there is no Moscow branch of the Sierra Club to trumpet it abroad. We do know, however, that the United States is engaged in a massive and costly effort to clean up and protect the environment.

From a statistical point of view, the distribution of income in European Communist countries is somewhat more equalitarian than it is in Western Europe. A person at the 25th income percentile in the Communist countries earns 82 per cent of the median income, as compared with his counterpart in the West who earns

76 per cent, according to Lindblom's figures; at the 95th percentile, the corresponding incomes are 184 per cent under Communism and 216 per cent in the West. Whether this represents a "great accomplishment" of Communism, as Lindblom asserts, depends less on what one makes of the numbers than on what one makes of the idea of statistical equality. Despite contrary appearances, scarcely anyone in America or Europe cares much about statistical equality. People do care about conditions that may, or may not, be related to statistical inequality, like subsistence-level incomes, unemployment, ethnic and sex discrimination, and worker alienation.

With the exception of unemployment, all these conditions afflict the Soviet Union and a good many of the other industrialized countries as well. An increase in statistical equality might mitigate them to some extent. But it might also aggravate them if greater equality were to diminish aggregate wealth and thereby increase alienation, discrimination, and the like. As for unemployment, we in the West mitigate this problem through social insurance, whereas the Soviets do so by obligatory job assignments. Lindblom euphemistically calls the Communist method "keeping a worker in the status of a participating member of the community." Whenever such methods—that is, welfare-linked work requirements—are proposed for this country, liberals call them intolerably coercive and a sham ("dead-end jobs").

Lindblom's judgments are scarcely better when applied to topics closer to home, like the alleged domination of government by "business." Very little evidence for this allegation is adduced, and most of it is irrelevant or misleading, such as a Republican Secretary of the Interior declaiming that the bicentennial year "is the year to wave the free-enterprise flag." Even when it can be shown that businessmen have a disproportionate influence on certain institutions or policy decisions (and this can be shown with no difficulty), it can also be shown that many other interests, such as labor unions, feminists, and even government bureaucracies, have carved out their own niches of power and privilege.

Lindblom's weak supporting evidence, however, is not nearly so disingenuous as his complete neglect of possible disconfirming evidence. Over the last twelve or thirteen years, business has been forced to accept a vast number of quite costly regulatory impositions in the areas of health and safety practices, environmental protection, hiring and promotion policies, and the disclosure of consumer information. Business interests consistently fought these impositions and almost as consistently lost; Lindblom hardly alludes to these developments.

The Indoctrination Hypothesis

Lindblom's case is weaker still with respect to the truly ingenuous proposition that business indoctrination of the public has created a climate of political opinion that tolerates business domination of government. His case rests largely on the fact that there is still widespread popular acceptance of the legitimacy of private property, business enterprise, and governmental self-restraint in the economy. To Lindblom, the defects in these ideas are so obvious that only a hypothesis of indoctrination can explain the resistance of other citizens to seeing them. But the indoctrination hypothesis is two-edged; one could as legitimately postulate that the citizenry sees things more clearly than Lindblom and that it is he, not they, who has succumbed to malign influences.

Of all the malefactions of business, creation of the corporate form of organization is for Lindblom the very worst. Lindblom's rhetoric is never more subtly barbed than when he writes that "leading corporations succeed in persuading consumers to buy automobiles with risk of carbon monoxide discharges into the interior of the passenger compartment, pesticides harmful to those who use them, . . . cosmetics and other drugstore products that do not perform as claimed, all kinds of goods with hidden or deliberately misstated credit charges. . . ." In fact, however, for complicated reasons having relatively little to do with conscience or morality, large corporations behave, on the average, in a *more* "socially responsible" way than small businesses with respect to worker safety, product quality, environmental protection, and affirmative action. And "leading" corporations, precisely because they have a stake in their reputations, are more reliable still.

Worse than overstatement, though, is Lindblom's insinuation of motives, as if corporate managers *wanted* consumers to fall ill or to become disgruntled with their purchases. Actions that end up harming some consumers generally derive from a decision that helps all consumers, namely, the decision to hold down cost and price. Lindblom's intentional neglect of the context in which such a decision is made is equivalent to saying that a drug company marketing ten million doses of Sabin vaccine intends to kill or disable ten people because the company knows that such side-effects show up statistically at the rate of about one in a million.

Lindblom concludes *Politics and Markets* with the contention that the large private corporation "does not fit" into "democratic theory and vision." But corporations face stiffer federal tax rates than most businesses or private citizens, and they are subject to much more extensive government regulation than lesser economic entities. Are they to be taxed and regulated without being allowed to participate in the democratic political process?

To be sure, corporate managers can participate in the political process by using other people's (shareholders') money. In this respect, though, corporate managers are identical to the leaders of many other large, and politically legitimate, organizations in American life, including labor unions, foundations, and government bureaucracies themselves. Corporations are major actors and major stakeholders, and they deserve political standing as such. If they do not fit Lindblom's theory of pluralist democracy, it is mainly his theory that needs to be revised.

An Alarmist View of Corporate Influence

ROYALL BRANDIS

A DISTINGUISHED SCHOLAR has written a book that is undistinguished and unscholarly.

The reader, if he accepts that judgment, need go no further; the reviewer, however, is obligated to evidence such a statement. First, *Politics and Markets* purports to be an interdisciplinary study of "... the fundamental questions about government and politics, about market systems, and about the relations between the two" (p. ix). In fact, it is a vicious attack, approaching hysteria at times, on democratic government and the free market system especially as these institutions have developed in the United States. It is presented in the guise of a balanced, scientific study of today's politico-economic systems. But the guise gets very thin at times. For example:

> It is difficult for a thoughtful liberal democrat to read Lenin or Mao without recognizing on some points a kinship of spirit. That they have given orders to imprison and to kill thousands, even millions, does not conclusively deny their humanitarianism any more conclusively than the massive civilian bombing of Germany in World War II, to say nothing of atomic bombing of Japan and the devastation of Vietnam, denies it for American political leaders. While we draw distinctions between the one and the other, and between one ethic and another, both groups of leaders claim to kill for humanitarian principles [p. 260].

ROYALL BRANDIS is professor of economics at the University of Illinois at Urbana-Champaign. This article is reprinted by permission from the "Southern Economic Journal," January 1979.

In addition to noting the inability to distinguish between international warfare and domestic repression of opposition political beliefs, the reader should also pay attention to the use of weasel words and phrases in the above quotation, i.e., "thoughtful," "on some points," "conclusively," and "we." The book abounds in similar cases. The liberal democrat who doesn't recognize a kinship of spirit to Lenin or Mao is, presumably, just not being thoughtful. And who is "we"? The author? Thoughtful liberal democrats? The book is peppered with others: "most noncommunist systems," "in some eyes," "many liberals" (p. 165); "thoughtful people perhaps believe" (p. 275); "for good or bad," "at least hypothetically" (p. 280), to give a few examples. If this were just a fuzzy style it would be irritating, not worth review mention; but it often happens that the fuzziness appears just when clarity would be most needed, if this were the scholarly study it purports to be.

A Confusion of Systems

Lindblom is careless about specifying the particular nation or group of nations he is describing as well as careless about pinning down the time period he is writing about. Since, in one classification, he divides all the world's political and economic systems into only three categories of which China and Cuba occupy one alone, it is obvious that confusion of systems can easily result. Thus, when he tells us, "even in an ostensibly democratic system, a police department sometimes uses harassment, blackmail, and assassination to establish authority over its hierarchical superiors" (p. 29), we are given no hint (and no citation) of to what nation(s) the reference is made.

Sometimes one piece of poor scholarship is used to support another. In a paragraph (pp. 205, 206) that gives no date, Lindblom says, "Schools and colleges have been particular targets of corporate opinion formation on the grand issues. For example, in the United States. . . ." A long quotation follows from a book by Grant McConnell published in 1966. McConnell footnotes the statement quoted by Lindblom, citing (without date or page reference), "U.S. Federal Trade Commission, *Utility Corporations*, No.

72A." This is a 1935 publication of 882 pages,† none of which, as well as I can determine, lend any support to McConnell's original statement, much less to Lindblom's reliance on the quoted passage forty-two years later to substantiate a sweeping statement about education (today?) in the United States.

It is not easy to untangle the confusion of words, meanings, and concepts presented by the author. First, consider the key word "polyarchy." Lindblom says, "Following recent precedent, we shall call the controls 'polyarchic,' meaning rule by many,[7] and a system that incorporates them a polyarchy rather than a democracy*'" (p. 132). Note 7 (found on p. 366) reads as follows in its entirety: "From the use of the term in Robert A. Dahl and Charles E. Lindblom, *Politics, Economics and Welfare* (New York: Harper & Brothers, 1953)." The asterisked footnote is at the bottom of page 132 and explains that "for convenience we will call the United States, the nations of Western Europe, and certain others polyarchies . . . ," but, Lindblom says, polyarchy is only one system of social control in those nations; the other systems are not given in the note.

One might be tolerant of such word coinage if it seemed to have some purpose, but, if it does, that purpose escaped me. One might suppose that polyarchy would have been contrasted with oligarchy and monarchy (or "uniarchy" if one wished both to coin a word and to ignore a legitimate meaning of "monarchy," namely, rule by one person—not necessarily called a king). Instead, "socialism" and "communism" are often used in the same classification scheme with "polyarchy" with a careless lack of distinction between the first two terms. On other occasions, the classification scheme is a three-fold one of "polyarchy," "authority," and "preceptoral system."

The logic of Lindblom's anti-democratic argument ranges from the sophistic to the sophomoric. An important element of his argument is that any evidence indicative of popular preference for

---

†The correct citation is: U.S. Senate, 70th Congress, 1st Session, Document 92, Part 72-A. *Utility Corporations*: Summary Report of the Federal Trade Commission to the Senate of the United States Pursuant to Senate Resolution No. 83, U.S. Government Printing Office, Washington: 1935.

democratic or polyarchic government should be rejected since it is, in reality, evidence of the success of business corporations in making the rest of us *think* we prefer democracy. Thus: "Perhaps the United States has no widely circulating radical newspaper because no wide audience wants it. But that is our very point" (p. 212). Or, "Consider the possibility that businessmen achieve an indoctrination of citizens so that citizens' volitions serve not their own interests but the interests of businessmen. Citizens then become allies of businessmen" (p. 202). And how is this indoctrination achieved? "Corporations employ all possible methods, overt and covert. The source of their communications is usually obscure. The message usually reaches the citizens indirectly in a news story or broadcast, a magazine article, a film, an editorial, a political speech, or a conversation. Only a small part of it comes explicitly from a business source" (p. 206). No rational criticism is likely to have much force against such a paranoiac view of life in the United States. Indeed, a critical review such as this one can only confirm Lindblom's belief that not even university faculty can escape the insidious influence of the corporation.

An Attempt to Prove Mind-Control

The author's techniques of obfuscation are transparent ones. He will, for example, devote an entire chapter (chapter 15) to an attempt to prove that business in the United States exercises mind-control over the American people so that they *think* they want what they don't *really* want and thus mistakenly support the economic arrangements which exist in this country. Yet, in the last paragraph of the chapter appear statements to the effect that things are not nearly so bad as in authoritarian systems and that they only look bad in the United States compared to an ideal democratic society. Presumably, the author is now in a position to argue that he has made an objective, even-handed analysis of conditions in the United States.

Or consider his use of quotation marks in a way familiar to anyone who has read undergraduate term papers. For example, with reference to modern China: "The communist 'new man' was to be achieved through preceptoral 'education'" (p. 277). In context it is clear that we are not to give the obvious meaning to "new man" or to "education." But what meaning, exactly, are we to give to them? "Education" we have been told earlier will be put in quotes because it covers "persuasion, information, indoctrination, instruction, propaganda, counseling, advice, exhortation, education, and thought control . . ." (p. 56). A word that means all that means nothing—or, rather, means whatever the user chooses to have it mean on any particular occasion.

What about "new man"? Is this irony? Is it a quotation (no source is given)? Is there a double meaning? The reader must decide for himself. The author has kept his options open.

'The Intellectually Guided Society'

If one struggles through all the rhetoric, through all the sophistic proofs of the correctness of the author's prejudices, through all the pseudo-objective analysis, he can perceive the author's message. It is that the hope of mankind lies in his hypothetical Model 1. And what is Model 1? "Model 1 might be called an intellectually guided society" (p. 248). "The model of the intellectually guided society, Model 1, specifies that some people in the society are wise and informed enough to ameliorate its problems and guide social change with a high degree of success" (p. 249). "In Model 1, ince some people *know* how to organize society, the test of an institution or policy is that it is correct" (p. 250, emphasis in the original). And, finally, "since it is knowledge rather than volition that guides society in Model 1, the intellectual elite is simultaneously a political elite" (p. 251). Now *there's* a thought to quicken the pulse of any sheltered academic. But we should also note that "in Model 1, problem-solving interactions [differences of opinion] are suppressed as a source of disorganization and trouble" (p. 255). The author says nothing about how the intellectual elite gets to be the political elite. A serious study of politico-economic systems would hardly have omitted so important a topic.

In the real world, according to Lindblom, both China and the U.S.S.R. approach the fulfillment of Model 1, but have not yet attained it. It is clear in Model 1 whose view prevails if the intellectual elite differs from the masses. What is not clear (or even mentioned) is what happens if members of the intellectual elite differ with each other. We know how Stalin settled his difference with Trotsky by sending an assassin to Mexico to put a pickax in his brain.

The naïveté is really a little sad. It is also a travesty on social science. One feels that the author simply does not comprehend the importance of the ideas of freedom of thought and of the inviolability of the individual. Any real world system or hypothetical model which rejects that theme represents retrogression, not advance, on mankind's long path to a truly civilized society.

How Powerful Is Business?

ITHIEL DE SOLA POOL

CHARLES LINDBLOM'S THESIS of the power of business in democratic societies is a familiar one: business exercises excessive power. I shall not argue for or against the point; I am not sure that I know whether business influence is too great, too small, or just about right. What I wish to evaluate is the logic of the argument.

First of all, Lindblom confuses business—namely, the for-profit sector that encompasses the large majority of the American workers—with a small group of top executives in large corporations. Sometimes he talks about one and sometimes the other, traveling between the two conceptions with marvelous ease.

Business, he asserts, exercises an influence quite different from that of other interest groups. It has far more influence than labor, or the intelligentsia, or the press, he says. But since we do not know which of his two conceptions of "business" he is using here, it is hard to judge whether the claim is true.

Lindblom argues that business exercises its power not only through economic blackmail and political shenanigans but also by somehow capturing the minds of the rest of us. Some sort of "false conscious-

ITHIEL DE SOLA POOL is Ruth and Arthur Sloan Professor of Political Science at the Massachusetts Institute of Technology, where he has taught for nearly three decades. He has written or edited several books in the areas of communications and public opinion, including "Talking Back: Citizen Feedback and Cable Technology" and "The Social Impact of the Telephone."

23

ness" (though he distinguishes his view in some details from Marx's use of that term) leads us to refrain from challenging the basic business viewpoint.

There is nothing remarkable in the argument as I have sketched it. It has appeared in thousands of tracts and articles over the past century and a half. It is the ABC of the radical critique of capitalist society. What distinguishes Lindblom's statement from 99 per cent of the rest is not the case or its accuracy but the sophistication with which he makes it.

Lindblom starts by flagging a fact that might be embarrassing to his case, namely, that "liberal democracy has arisen only in nations that are market-oriented" (*Politics and Markets*, p. 5). He sets up four categories of societies:

1. market-oriented and "polyarchic" (his word for democratic),
2. market-oriented and authoritarian,
3. centrally planned and polyarchic,
4. centrally planned and authoritarian.

Category 3 is empty of examples; there are no polyarchies in countries without a market economy.

Having proceeded in proper rhetorical fashion to present the strongest argument against his case, Lindblom now tells us we should not fear that if we move away from a market orientation, democracy (or polyarchy) will be undermined. There is, he says, "no compelling reason for the two to be tied together." How does he support that? One might expect that, having shown a strong historical correlation, he would have to go on to show that the correlation was a historical accident. If there is a strong indication that centrally planned economies erode the very basis of democratic decision-making, then we should demand strong evidence that the causal relation was an illusion before we consider experimenting with central planning.

But instead of evidence Lindblom offers a brief semantic comment. He explains that the facts to which the term "polyarchy" refers are different from the facts to which "market-oriented" refers; one refers to the economy, the other to the polity. Since the two definitions pertain to different spheres, we need not fear that we can't have one without the other.

A less compelling argument is hard to imagine. We can certainly agree that a term referring to the economy and a term referring to the polity cannot be synonymous. But Lindblom has conceded that there is an empirical relationship between these two things—i.e., a relationship not in the realm of logic but in history. He does nothing to help us understand why we should not assume this relationship to be one of cause and effect.

If it were true that political controls over market allocations brought no unintended consequences, this would be a happy world. The market, as Lindblom among others has helped us to understand, is just one way of making economic decisions, and it has both advantages and disadvantages. Indeed, the whole political process in market-oriented democracies is devoted to correcting unacceptable results of the working of the market. Majority rule is a legitimate means for imposing public control on undesirable market outcomes. But to impose controls on the market has bad as well as good consequences, loss of some freedom being among the bad ones.

Public control, Lindblom notes, has rarely been considered a supreme end in its own right. The most desirable arrangement is that each person be able to do as he wishes. Only in situations where that creates difficulties for others is there reason for the majority to impose its preferences on the minority.

Are Collective Problems Growing?

Lindblom understands that historically democracy has been viewed not as an end in itself but as a means to liberty, and he offers us little reason to retreat from that view. At one point he mentions a series of great public issues that obviously call for collective decision, such as environmental degradation and the avoidance of atomic holocaust. But, although he asserts that we are in a new era in which collective problems are of growing weight relative to the ones that can best be handled by individual decisions, he offers no evidence on this point.

A number of factors operating in the contemporary world favor a withering away of central decision-making. One is the increasing affluence in industrial societies. More and more people have s accumulated resources. To have money in the bank is a prime condition for individual independence. Slavery, feudalism, sharecropping, and various other forms of personal dependence reflected the historical fact that in most societies most people could not live even a few weeks on their own accumulated resources.

Another factor favoring pluralistic decision-making is international geographic mobility. Single nations may have socialistic tendencies within them, leading to growing government controls, but increasingly business operates on a global basis, locating activities wherever conditions are most favorable.

A more important factor favoring individual decision-making is the technology of electronics. The use of computers and other modern electronic systems permits the individualization of what were formerly mass activities.

Whether Marx was right in expecting post-industrial developments to lead to the withering away of the state, or whether Lindblom is right in expecting more collectivism, is an open question. Lindblom does not attempt to prove his claim. On this as on so many other points he proceeds by dicta, not data.

For Lindblom (as also for socialists over the past 150 years) the most decisive reason for turning over more economic decisions to the political authorities is dissatisfaction with the way businessmen are making those decisions. Whether the language chosen is Marx's phrase "capitalist exploitation" or such terms as "200 families" and "robber barons" or Lindblom's more scholarly words about the "extraordinarily disproportionate influence" of a "dominating minority," the argument is the same. Businessmen are portrayed as the dominant elite of our society.

In some respects, of course, the portrayal is true. The great majority of our labor force is in the for-profit sector, and the greatest part of our GNP is produced by that sector. Since for-profit enterprise is the most prevalent activity, persons in decision-making positions in that sector do play in our society. Collectively, they provide the major activity. ese business leaders are not democratically r worse, our society has chosen to rely more on corrective processes of competition and on a pluralism of self-constituted groups than on representative election, except in the government(A good case can be made for the introduction of democratic processes at various places in business. Experiments with worker participation in some areas of decision-making are an example. But the basic principle of letting private entrepreneurs make their own decisions, corrected and chastened by the marketplace, is certainly a sound one for much activity. The case for representative government in that one organization to which willy-nilly we all belong, the state, does not hold for Mom and Pop's grocery store, or for Edwin Land's Polaroid Corporation, or even for General Motors. If we do not like what General Motors does we can deal with Ford, or even with Saab.)

The 'Grand Issues'

Lindblom recognizes that businessmen do not agree about everything. However, there are, he says, certain "grand issues" on which "business tends to speak with one voice." Business influence over the media and over government keeps these "grand issues" from coming under public discussion; the issues are kept out of political debate.

One can readily agree with Lindblom that the market-oriented democracy has some largely unchallenged consensual views. As he says, "a set of unifying beliefs that assert the virtues of the fundamentals of social organization will be found in any stable society" (p. 230). But when Lindblom starts to list these fundamental and unchallenged assumptions, one is aghast. Issues that he says are kept out of the political debate in the market-oriented democracies of North America and Western Europe include: the privileged position of business, the association of private enterprise with political democracy, preservation of the status quo in income distribution, close consultation between business and government, and the restriction of union demands to those consistent with business profitability.

Now really! I wish Lindblom would name the country he is talking about, the one in which the privileged position of business is excluded from political debate; where no politician wins votes by proposing to soak the rich; where there are no labor or socialist parties; where books like Lindblom's *Politics and Markets* are never published; where hardly any young intellectuals read and discuss the works of Marx; where there is no consumer movement; where there are no magazines that can be described as belonging to the left; where the left is not critical of business. What is the country in which income distribution is not a political issue; in which there is no debate in the parliament about such matters as income taxes and capital-gains taxes; in which social security payments are not a significant expenditure or a widely discussed political matter? If it is the United States that Lindblom has in mind when he says that close consultation between business and government is kept from becoming a political issue, one wonders how he would explain the press attention given to such news items as Bert Lance's bank loans or the campaign contributions to CREEP (the Nixon reelection committee). And would he say that Senate committees dealing with confirmation show little interest in the investment portfolios of rich appointees to public office?

It is perfectly plain that the central issues of politics in Western democracies are precisely those of the distribution of property and wealth. The dividing line in most countries is between a socialist party that defines its fundamental goal as the socialization of the means of production and a capitalist party. Although there is no significant socialist party in the United States, the fundamental political issues have nonetheless been the power of business and the distribution of wealth. Far from being excluded from politics, these issues are at its heart.

True, the socialists have not succeeded in displacing the market-based system in any democracy, even those in which they have held office. Perhaps their programs are so impracticable that people see through them, or perhaps when their programs are tried they turn out to be catastrophic failures. But Lindblom's case is not that somehow business has won its battle to stay alive as the major sector in the economy; his argument is that it has not even had a battle to fight because it has captured men's minds. That is clearly absurd. Orthodox Marxists who talk about class struggle (while also indulging in myths of sorts) are far closer to the truth than is Lindblom's fantasy of a society in which business is so strong that it is not even politically embattled.

There are, of course, in market-oriented democracies, some values that are truly consensual and are removed from political debate. Among the values upon which consensus smiles are the family, the nation-state, peace as a fundamental goal, individual integrity, individual property, work, and comfortable living standards. On each of these there is occasional dissent, but it is of no lasting political consequence. No one would argue that these items of political consensus constitute mere "business ideology." Indeed, the very reason that they are items of consensus is that they cut across the beliefs of all major sectors of the population.

Why Government Protects Business

What remains, then, of Lindblom's thesis that business is not just one interest group among others, like labor, the intelligentsia, or the press? Something does. Business, if by that we mean the for-profit sector, is by far the largest sphere of activity in the society, employing most people, generating most of the GNP. It is certainly true, as Lindblom tells us, that government officials are usually protective of business activity—as they are of the activity of smaller sectors such as non-profit institutions and the press. Any responsible government wants the major institutions of its society to work well. Government leaders are happy when businessmen invest, when new jobs are created, and when trade expands, and they regard it as a legitimate aim of policy to promote such developments. They are receptive to suggestions from business about means to achieve such goals, though they may be highly suspicious of possible personal motives as they listen to individual businessmen.

To the extent that government desires to see the major sector of the economy progress, it is, as Lindblom emphasizes, protective of and beholden to business. It is not free to act with irresponsible disregard for the interests of business.

But from that obvious point Lindblom jumps to some extraordinary statements about government and "businessmen." Businessmen, he maintains, are, apart from government office-holders, the most powerful persons in our society. They have a special relationship with public officials; they control vast amounts of money; they dominate the media and other institutions. Presumably by "businessmen" Lindblom means the top officials of the Fortune 500 corporations—vice-presidents and above—plus a certain number of very wealthy investors. Clearly the picture he is drawing does not include the rental agent of an apartment house, or the owner of the local laundry, or a traveling salesman, though all these persons would call themselves businessmen.

In fact, of course, there is a distribution of power in every sector. It makes no sense to compare the power of the president of the Chase Manhattan Bank with that of a college professor or an unpublished poet; yet that is the way the argument is often made. If we look at comparable levels in various professional areas, the differences are not very great. James Reston, at the power peak of journalism, is probably a more powerful man than the head of the Chase Bank. The president of Harvard is certainly in the league. Charles Lindblom, an eminently successful professor, is not in the same league of power, but he is certainly more influential in American life than any but a couple of thousand top businessmen; few businessmen can blow as frightening a trumpet as he can. And the same is true for the top few hundred Washington or foreign correspondents, columnists, and editors.

The Special Interests of Businessmen

In Lindblom's vocabulary, then, "businessmen" means the top executives of corporations and major money managers. These persons, like any other distinguishable set, have certain special interests that include, but are not identical with, the general health of the institutions that they head. They are in that respect no different from any other employees. Like union members they want "more" for themselves, while at the same time they have an interest in seeing their firms succeed. The personal concerns of top corporation executives are focused on such matters as taxes, SEC rules, bonuses, and pensions. Bankers and investors have slightly different special interests, though all of them share a general concern for business growth, or what is generally called prosperity.

The special situation of corporate executives in the United States and how it differs from that of capitalists in the classic sense deserves a lot more attention than it gets from Lindblom's broad brush. Corporate executives in the United States today are highly paid but insecure employees. They can get rich by the standards of a college professor or government official, but not by the standards of those with great fortunes. People with AT&T, by most measures the largest corporation in the country, are fond of pointing out that no one in the company ever made a fortune. The corporation is essentially a bureaucracy, with high salaries at the top but no opportunity to make what a successful—smart and lucky—buccaneer on the stock or commodities market can make.

The reader may be tempted to object that AT&T is a special case because it is a regulated industry; but the fact that the government does regulate that and other businesses serves as further evidence that the government is not a servant of business.

The people who have influence are the ones who can come in and say, "I speak for 50,000 jobs." They may be corporate executives, or bankers, or hired managers of investment funds, such as pension funds. They may be union leaders. When they speak for their own self-interest, their credibility and influence is small. Often they speak for themselves under the guise of speaking for the sector of the economy that they represent, as when they ask for less discouraging tax rates at the higher levels on the grounds of stimulating investment. But their greatest influence comes when they really speak for workers in their sector, with no self-interest except the general interest that any leader has in the success of his institution.

In this respect businessmen do not differ from union leaders, educators, and people from the mass media. But Lindblom fails to see that. He talks about the power and influence of business and translates that into the power and influence of businessmen in serving their self-interest. Then he talks about unions, but he never translates the power of unions into the power of union leaders in serving their self-interest; he somehow equates their power with the interests of the workers. He talks about the media and the intellectuals as though they are somehow elevated in their concerns in a way different from businessmen. Few congressmen would agree that either the educational establishment or the media fight any less fiercely for their interests than do businessmen. Those of us who argue for the national importance of spending more on research differ not at all from a businessman arguing for more favorable treatment of his industry. Both are serving a mixture of legitimate special and general interests.

Lindblom compiles a long list of supposedly unique features of the political influence of business, but the only one in which business really differs from the rest is one that Lindblom does not mention: its aggregate percentage of our economy. He claims that business is the only interest group that finances its political activities with other people's money, i.e., out of the treasuries of business. But who finances the trips of academics to Washington to sit on panels about national research needs? Who financed journalists who exposed the Nixon administration's attacks on the networks? Every organized institution uses its treasury to promote policies that are in its interest, and in a free society it should not be otherwise.

Initiator or Saboteur?

Lindblom comes up with another revelation, that all government regulation of business is a sham. But he tries to have it both ways. First he describes how business resists new regulatory legislation, uses back-room influence in both executive and legislative branches to weaken it, and sabotages it to some extent when it is enacted. No doubt there are examples of all such activities; to some extent that is what is known as politics. But if affected businesses fight regulation so savagely, then how are we to believe Lindblom's other argument, that regulation is really initiated by business to achieve special privileges, and only camouflaged as action in defense of the people? "A new group of historians," Lindblom tells us, "believe they are finding evidence of a common pattern. Policy is changed in response to business controls and is then paraded as democratic reform." He cites revisionist historians on food and drug legislation, municipal reform, and banking reform, and then says: "To none of these reforms was popular demand an important contributor" (p. 191).

Once more, there is a germ of truth to these discoveries. The old naïve view was that business was a unified devil that brave reformers subjected to regulation in the public interest, though sometimes, admittedly, business later recaptured the regulatory agency and reversed its true purpose. But the reality was always more complex. When there were abuses that significant elements of the public wanted regulated, some of the more "responsible" elements of business saw that it would be in their interest to have these abuses controlled. Indeed, they sometimes even saw ways to gain monopoly advantages out of the regulation. So the real fight was not the people against business but some public interests aligned with some business interests against other public and business interests. Now the new naïve view comes along: it is really business that is pulling all the strings; reformist movements have played no role in "reform."

Two decades ago I collaborated on a study of business activities in regard to foreign trade legislation (Raymond A. Bauer, Ithiel de Sola Pool, and Lewis A. Dexter, *American Business and Public Policy*, Chicago: Aldine, Atherton, 1963). I began with no particular presuppositions about how business operated in politics, except for an assumption that businessmen would fight hard in politics for their particular economic interests.

With research came some surprising discoveries. In the first place, businessmen's economic interests were rarely clear to them: even when expectations could be clearly defined there were many different ways in which they could use their money and resources. Second, being specialists in the private sector, businessmen were often extremely maladroit and uncomfortable in the unfamiliar world of the public sector. Third, in the interaction between businessmen and politicians, politicians mobilized businessmen to serve the politicians' interests as often as businessmen mobilized politicians to serve business interests. Fourth, conflicts of interest within business often served to preclude action by major business interests, while quite minor business interests might prove effective if not checked by such conflicts. (Lindblom cites this book only to document the point that legislators use research provided by businesses and trade associations. He makes no mention of the main points we were making—that business interests moderate their stands to win this sort of acceptance from politicians, and that the result is two-way influence.)

In the end, the conclusion has to be that the process of politics is a complex set of two-way influences, with constantly shifting alliances. No one wins all and no one loses all. The attempt to reduce this to a simple theory of hidden monolithic control is bound to be wrong.

And it is not only wrong but also dangerous. Lindblom uses this theory for an attack on the corporation. Clearly there can be many arguments about the rights and wrongs of current corporate structure or legal status. But the premise from which we need to start in a free society is that of freedom of association. If a group of persons wish to pool their resources to engage in an enterprise, society should encourage, not discourage, them. It should certainly not subject them to more control than necessary.

Lindblom's attack on the corporation is an attack not on particular abuses that may occur from time to time but on the basic idea of freedom of association in a free society.

Democracy and the Corporation

JAMES Q. WILSON

IT'S NO SURPRISE THAT academics in this country have been generally suspicious of business or that in a time like this, when general public confidence in the corporation has fallen, the expressions of hostility grow sharper. But there's rarely been a better example of this than Charles E. Lindblom's book *Politics and Markets: The World's Political-Economic Systems*.

In the great tradition of political economy, Mr. Lindblom, a professor at Yale University and one of our most distinguished theorists of politics, has set himself the task of clarifying the basic features of political and economic systems and their interactions in capitalist and Communist societies, and his attempt is likely to be influential.

The book that results is essentially in three parts: one brilliant, the second illuminating, the third an embarrassment.

The brilliance is to be found in Mr. Lindblom's analysis of the logic of the market and of its opposite, planning—subjects to which he has devoted a lifetime of scholarly reflection. Unlike many critics of capitalism, he sees markets as essential to any economic order and understands why comprehensive—he calls it "synoptic"—planning cannot replace them, though in every soci-

JAMES Q. WILSON is Henry Lee Shattuck Professor of Government at Harvard University. This article is reprinted by permission from the January 11, 1978, issue of the "Wall Street Journal" (© 1978 Dow Jones & Company; all rights reserved).

ety the attempt has been made. The imperfections of the market are carefully stated, and the efforts of governments and business to subvert it duly noted. Whatever its defects, however, Mr. Lindblom points out that the market occupies a remarkable place in any generalized statement about political institutions: though not all market-oriented systems are democratic, every democratic system is also market-oriented.

The promised explanation of this extraordinary fact is never wholly forthcoming, though in another section of the book Mr. Lindblom notes the historical circumstances that linked the growth of democracy and markets in some countries during the eighteenth and nineteenth centuries. More revealing is his account of how China, Cuba, and the Soviet Union have struggled to find a viable alternative to markets: bureaucracy in the U.S.S.R., "moral incentives" in China and Cuba, the reliance on rationing in all three. Mr. Lindblom sets forth the available data—suspect, to be sure, but circumspectly used—on the results of these efforts in terms of income distribution and economic growth.

But the central part of the book, and what appears to be the central point as well, is Mr. Lindblom's discussion of the "close but uneasy relationship between private enterprise and democracy." The argument, stripped of its (minor) qualifications, can be simply stated: The large private corporation is a threat to democracy and, indeed, has no place in democratic theory.

But if markets are essential, if comprehensive planning is impossible, and if all democratic systems are market-oriented, how can the corporation be such a villain? The answer, says Mr. Lindblom, is two-fold: First, the corporation is an authoritarian structure in which control is vested in those who own property rather than those who supply labor. Second, it is a locus of political privilege that distorts and even corrupts the democratic process. This distortion results from the fact that businessmen have superior organization, enjoy disproportionate access to elected officials, dispose of vast political contributions (legal and illegal), control the appointment of government regulators, and are capable of molding "human volitions" through advertising, ownership of the mass media, and influence on school curricula.

Stated baldly, this reads like a burlesque of the actual political position of business. Indeed, whereas the first part of this book is logically exact and the latter part empirically thorough, this section reads as though it were a political tract from the 1930s, a pastiche of muckraking journalism, revisionist history, and the selective use of academic studies. Advertising is called "thought control," the academic profession is described as espousing "the beliefs of the favored (i.e., business) class," child-rearing practices and even the love of competitive sports are said to support a respect for authority and property that helps the favored (again, the business) class, and so on.

The contrary hypothesis is easily stated. Since the 1930s, and especially since the 1960s, the drift of public policy has been increasingly hostile to business. Public confidence in the corporation has fallen (indoctrination?), the national media are increasingly critical, capital formation is inhibited by taxes and inflationary policies, the profit margins of corporations have declined, social and economic regulations proliferate almost faster than the Federal Register can print them, antitrust prosecution, though perhaps not as effective as one might desire, falls more heavily on firms here than elsewhere, and the barriers to public control of traditionally private industries (hospitals, railroads, even medical practice) are dropping rapidly.

Do Resources Bestow Power?

The essential difference between Mr. Lindblom's theory and the alternative stated above is that his imputes power to an institution or class on the basis of the resources it possesses, while the other attempts to measure power on the basis of who wins and who loses. The fallacy of the Lindblom view is well known to every student of politics: One cannot *assume* that the disproportionate possession of certain resources (money, organization, status) leads to the disproportionate exercise of political power. Everything depends on whether a resource can be converted into power, and at what rate and at what price. That, in turn, can only be learned by finding out who wins and who loses.

Since Mr. Lindblom is quite familiar with this issue, one wonders why he chose to ignore it. He might reply that he did not—that he cited many cases of actual business control over public acts like regulatory policies. But one discovers that he relies for his evidence on revisionist (i.e., neo-Marxist) historians whose studies have been seriously—in my view, often fatally—criticized. And the conflicting evidence on these issues is not discussed.

Mr. Lindblom might also respond, and does, that business may lose on "secondary" issues but not on the "grand" issues of public ownership and control. But this argument is both vague and myopic: What exactly are the "grand" issues and why have corporations lost on what appear to be such issues in some countries (Sweden?) where "crucial factors" like child-rearing practices and advertising practices are presumably quite similar to those in this country?

Or, finally, he might return the challenge: Surely one cannot argue that business is impotent, that its political resources are valueless, or that it would spend millions on advertising if it did not think it worthwhile? And he could be right, to the extent that no doubt corporations do have power. But the question is on what kinds of issues, under what circumstances?

For a long time, business could block environmental controls; now they cannot. Why? They have great power, it would appear, in maintaining the favorable tax treatment of capital gains, but not in lowering the corporate tax rate. Why? They lose on most OSHA regulations but win (usually) on maritime subsidies. Why?

Clearly, some distinctions are in order. But even more, some research is in order. This book is destined, I think, to have a great intellectual influence. And it fails in that part where evidence rather than logical analysis is most necessary. It is an armchair view of American politics and stereotyped from the outset: The only actors on the stage are elected politicians and business firms, so Mr. Lindblom sees the latter as being the principal constraint on the former.

But to a participant in politics, and even to most observers, the full list of actors is much larger and the constraints far more complex. The student reading this book will learn nothing of the professions, the bureaucracy, the courts, or the public-interest law firms, and next to nothing of the mass media, intellectuals, "experts," universities, and foundations that have such a large effect on American public life. It is a pity, because in the past we have learned so much from Professor Lindblom.

Business, Government, the Public: Who Manipulates Whom?

PAUL J. HALPERN

CHARLES LINDBLOM'S ARGUMENT about the role of corporate power in Western democracies can be reduced to three central propositions. First, all societies based on market economies need to offer inducements to business interests to produce goods and services. Second, business interests receive more inducements in the form of autonomy and privileges than are really necessary to sustain a healthy market system. Third, the political role of the business sphere is incompatible with democratic theory because it enables business to manipulate public preferences and to evade publicly sanctioned controls on its conduct. Lindblom holds that market-oriented democracies fall significantly short of the ideals of democracy and do not apply to business the amount of regulation necessary to prevent a future global catastrophe of technological origins.

The usual response of democratic pluralists to the argument that business has excessive influence in Western democracies is to point to the numerous political issues on which business interests have either lost or had to compromise greatly. The problem with this approach is that the theorists of business dominance are willing to state their case at such a broad level of abstraction that it is difficult

PAUL J. HALPERN is a regulatory reform consultant in Washington, D.C. He has a Ph.D. from Harvard. He formerly taught at UCLA and American University and was assistant director of the American Bar Association's Commission on Law and the Economy.

to disprove. Lindblom is no different. He offers a list of "secondary issues" on which business interests conflict with one another and are therefore not dominant. These "secondary issues" that he is willing to concede include much of the agenda of American politics today—"educational policy, tax reform, foreign policy, energy conservation, and space exploration" (*Politics and Markets*, p. 233). What matter to him are the "grand issues"—retention of the private enterprise system itself, business autonomy, maintenance of the current distribution of wealth—on which, he says, there is a consensus among business interests that is imposed on the rest of us through influence-peddling or indoctrination.

Argued in this broadly abstract way, parts of the business-dominance theory are more trivial than wrong. Business interests do perform very important economic functions in society and are therefore given significant inducements and considerable political access by most politicians in economically advanced nations. This is as true in the Soviet Union, where these producer interests are nationalized, as in the United States, where they are not; it is not a point worth debating. Capitalist societies do favor capitalist institutions of private enterprise and private property. Again, this is hardly surprising and not a matter for debate.

What *is* worth debating is *why* capitalist societies such as the United States favor contemporary capitalism rather than a more rigidly controlled economy of either the market-oriented or the socialist variety. Lindblom's thesis is that the continued support for capitalism results from indoctrination. That thesis will be the focal point of this essay.

Because those who favor radical change of one kind or another in the economic system cannot bring themselves to admit that the public might really be opposed to such change, they almost always argue that the public will is defeated by some undemocratic device such as business lobbying (broadly defined) or by a "false consciousness" created by political and psychological manipulation. One obvious response to these comments is that the public simply does not want government regulation to proceed at a faster pace or to undertake a fundamental restructuring of the economic system because it genuinely likes the material rewards that the capitalist system is providing. Lindblom briefly considers this argument and dismisses it this way:

> To be sure, the electorate in a polyarchy [democracy] wants a high level of employment and other satisfying performance from businessmen. Its frequent passivity might be taken to imply an approval for many of the privileges of businessmen so long as business goes on producing. But the particular demands that businessmen make on government are communicated to government officials in ways other than through the electoral process and are largely independent of and in conflict with the demands that the electorate makes [p. 190].

One could easily find data to support the view that the interests of the electorate and the interests of business conflict: Between 1962 and 1978 alone more than thirty new regulatory programs were signed into law in the United States; the mass media carry stories about corporate corruption, injuries caused by consumer products, unhealthful working conditions; Congress holds endless hearings on proposals for structural reform of the corporate system; the universities and churches attack corporate behavior. Although Lindblom incorrectly considers all this anti-business activity to be somewhat trivial compared to pro-business "indoctrination," it can certainly be used to support an argument that the public sounds more hostile to than appreciative of contemporary capitalism. It is also true, as Lindblom notes, that not all regulatory statutes have been enforced to the letter of the law. In his own exaggerated words, "there is for the United States an impressive record of reforms being turned away from their ostensible polyarchically [democratically] chosen purposes" (p. 191).

One response to all of this is to point out just how much reform of the capitalist system has occurred over the last hundred years and how much regulation has been added in the last two decades. During the past hundred years, labor unions and the right to strike have grown to be powerful countervailing forces to business on worker-related issues. Apart from public utilities, monopolies have disappeared from the economy. The laws of product liability have been liberalized to protect the consumer. Federal and state agencies regulate every aspect of the production and distribution processes. Minimum-wage laws help the workers. During the

1960s and 1970s, several dozen new regulatory laws were enacted, while old laws were being enforced with new vigor as a result of the consumer movement. A truly impressive transformation has taken place from the earlier era of laissez-faire.

Change Through Evolution

Moreover, this transformation was democratically initiated, and some Marxists admit it is responsible for the continued survival of capitalism. The change, evolutionary rather than revolutionary, has fundamentally altered the system, even if it has not gone far enough to suit Lindblom. His ultimate point is that as long as there is any discrepancy between the amount of economic regulation that the public appears to want—as evidenced in current debate and in the laws that are on the books—and the amount that is actually in force, this discrepancy must be due to business control.

However, it is not clear that this discrepancy is really very significant, given the amount of change that has already occurred. Furthermore, the public debate and the laws on the books do not always represent the majority viewpoint. To a degree Lindblom recognizes this fact. He writes that on secondary issues majorities "are often dominated by a minority or a coalition of minorities. Or they are simply ignored by officials who are often not aware what the majority wishes on secondary issues" (p. 233). However, his insight is one-sided. The only potential examples he provides of this phenomenon are in the area of regulatory laws such as food and drug inspection, which some historians believe were principally backed by businesses that had a financial incentive to favor regulation. Leaving aside the question whether this is an accurate portrayal of legislative history, Lindblom uses these examples to try to show why some regulatory laws are not so tough or so effectively administered as the majority wishes.

But another possible interpretation, especially for regulatory statutes enacted during the 1960s and 1970s, is that a liberal minority is responsible for the laws' being *more* strict in language and *more* stringently enforced than the public as a whole would like. This same minority could also cause the public debate at times to be more anti-business in sentiment than the majority really feels. I am referring here to the influence of those upper-middle-class professionals, primarily in the social sciences and non-profit institutions, who have a vested interest in government regulations, an antipathy toward large corporations and materialistic values, and the intellectual and financial resources to gain for themselves a disproportionate influence within the majority party in this country and within the mass media.

During the last two decades this class of persons had its power base in the mass media and the federal agencies as well as in Congress. But its role in Congress is crucial. The Democratic party controlled Congress for forty-four of the last forty-nine years; it was able to control the committee and subcommittee chairman-ships that are crucial to issue-creation and issue-resolution in American politics. As the power of middle-class professionals grew within the Democratic party, it also grew within the congres-sional power structure. The result was a wave of legislative hear-ings and investigations on consumer and environmental matters and corporate reform that in the 1970s resulted in the greatest regulation of business since the New Deal. This development was certainly aided by a muckraking press and by political support, both open and covert, from federal agencies. But the party that controls the chairmanships of congressional committees has a vast power over the agenda of American domestic politics. Even the President, in announcing his legislative program, is usually borrow-ing issues that have been created or made popular by congressional initiatives.

To be sure, many of the new regulatory measures enacted in the last decade were supported by lopsided roll-call votes characteris-tic of "motherhood" issues, where even conservative Democrats and Republicans voted with the environmental and consumer forces. Such large majorities may represent a true public consen-sus. But they could also represent what only appears to be a consensus, a minority view given disproportionate influence by the sensational treatment of business-related matters in congressional hearings and in the mass media. This is even more of a possibility if one is focusing on the current political debate rather than on the laws already on the books. At any given time the political debate may be dominated by a vocal minority, its views amplified by influential mass media whose leaders share those views.

The only analysis of social class that appears in *Politics and Markets* is an argument that many people outside the upper classes identify with upper-class goals because the institutions of American society favor upper-class persons. Lindblom is silent about the countervailing tendency of many upper-class and middle-class persons to identify with the goals of the poor, and to reject contemporary capitalism in favor of a more rigidly controlled economic system—a trend that is very significant in American politics and one of the most important political developments of the twentieth century. This neglect, though only one example of the one-sidedness of Lindblom's presentation, is a particularly significant example.

'Passivity' as a Statement

There is another response to Lindblom even if, for the sake of argument, one grants that the current laws represent majority rather than minority public opinion. What Lindblom calls the "frequent passivity" of the public in the face of any discrepancies that exist between regulatory realities and the laws on the books could represent a form of majority opinion. The public may realize that rigidly enforced regulatory laws are costly not only to business firms but also to the consumer. Health and safety regulations increase production and paperwork costs, and much of this increase is passed on to the consumer in the form of higher prices or lower quality. In addition, the more of a social cost such as pollution one tries to eliminate through regulation, generally the higher the per-unit cost of the regulatory program.

When regulatory laws are enacted, however, the focus is rarely on the costs of regulation. Politicians do not like to put an explicit value on a human life, though implicitly they must do so all the time. Instead, the political debate is heavy with ethical content and symbolic issues. As Charles L. Schultze points out in *The Public Use of Private Interest,* the logic of the political process is to view societal problems as "crises" that demand "urgent" action. This is necessarily the way one gains visibility for an issue and mobilizes political support for proposed legislation.

The result generally is the enactment of laws that demand large and immediate changes, even though this is much more costly than a more gradual plan based on a well-conceived research program and a careful balancing of costs and benefits. And then loopholes are discovered and postponements develop as the true costs of some regulatory programs become evident to those responsible for administering them. The implementation of programs sometimes lags behind the goals stated in the statute, because politicians and administrators know the public does not want to pay exceedingly high costs. Although individual companies often lobby to put off enforcement as long as possible, lags in enforcement are ultimately attributable to the resistance of the group that eventually pays for all new laws—the wage-earning and tax-paying public. If a president and his appointees are closely identified with regulatory policies that are costly to business and the public, this identification may even contribute to his defeat at the polls as public sentiment turns against stronger regulation. The 1980 election is a case in point.

If this view of the political process is correct (and I acknowledge that, like Lindblom's alternative, it contains some speculative assumptions), then the occasional reluctance of the legislative and executive branches of government to push for tougher enforcement of regulatory laws or for larger regulatory budgets represents a legitimate public desire to minimize the direct and indirect costs of regulation, just as the law itself represents a legitimate public desire to improve the quality of life. The public is ambivalent. When it is asked for its opinion on symbolic and moral issues, or the worthiness of consumer and environmental goals in the abstract, it responds favorably. Later, when it gives its opinion on increased taxes and increased prices, it is not so enthusiastic, particularly if the increases are significant. To be sure, some public opinion polls indicate that in theory the public is willing to pay more for products that are environmentally safe. But in practice, as costs have increased, people have voted in the political and economic marketplaces for a somewhat different trade-off between consumer protection and income protection. There is no reason why one should assume that public attitudes on substantive goals are genuine while public attitudes on costs are phony.

One can hardly expect Lindblom to be sensitive to the political implications of these cost pressures since he seems to think that the costs fall on producers rather than on consumers. In addition, he is reluctant to acknowledge that the costs of regulation are significant.

A Silence in the Electorate

Lindblom uses what debate does exist on business-related issues as evidence of a discrepancy between public wants and political realities, but he also feels that such anti-business discussion is less than one should expect. Therefore in the second half of his analysis, the tables are turned. He asks, "Why do we not see more frequent electoral demands for, say, corporate reform, curbs on monopoly, income redistribution, or even central planning?" (p. 192). He notes that in Europe there is a receptivity to radical reforms "unmatched in the United States" (p. 212), even if Western European democracies have never seriously tried central planning of the production process. Presumably we are to conclude that this difference in electoral and public debate between Europe and the United States is due to a greater degree of business domination in the United States. However, as Louis Hartz noted over twenty years ago in *The Liberal Tradition in America,* the differences between the old world and the new are rooted in different political traditions. Lacking a feudal past against which to react, Americans are less likely to develop a socialist future. Moreover, the commitment of Americans to a liberal, acquisitive, and materialistic culture preceded the development of modern advertising techniques and the large corporation.

Despite these facts, Lindblom believes that indoctrination of the public by business interests through the mass media, the schools, the churches, and political institutions is prevalent in America since propaganda tends to reinforce rather than to change the preferences or "volitions" of citizens. Thus even if public attitudes originate elsewhere, indoctrination by business can be blamed for reinforcing the status quo. Lindblom is aware that such "indoctrination" is common in Communist systems, but he feels that in the West it conflicts with democratic ideals.

Playing Down the Hostility

In discussing the influence of the mass media on individual opinions, Lindblom completely ignores the studies that show a lack of significant effects. His treatment of opinion studies on equality of opportunity is also very narrow. But there are more basic objections to be made to Lindblom's analysis of indoctrination. One is his downplaying of the very evidence of hostility to business interests that earlier he finds so significant. For example, the fact that "more undergraduates read Marx than Adam Smith" (p. 213) is acknowledged but considered evidence only that "polyarchal politics is never quite a closed circle" (p. 213). If one looks at how the mass media, print media, schools, and churches portray business institutions, it is hard to conclude that anti-business attitudes are just a drop in the bucket of American culture. The rhetoric may not be in Marxist terms, but it is decidedly anti-business. It presents a strong countervailing force to any pro-business "indoctrination" that occurs in the United States.

A more basic problem with Lindblom's analysis of "indoctrination" is his assumption that if no pro-business "propaganda" occurred, American society, since it is a democracy, would naturally adopt more radical approaches to economic regulation or a significantly more equal distribution of wealth. In fact, there is no reason to assume this. The arithmetic of democratic politics does not mean that the "have-nots" always outnumber the haves. Therefore there is no reason to assume that the poor have the voting strength to force radical changes in income distribution.

America is a predominantly middle-class society. Its economic system has generated more wealth and a higher standard of living for the average citizen than the system of any other society of comparable size has done. As James Q. Wilson has noted, one result of having a middle-class majority is that middle-class people, rather than the poor, are often the chief beneficiaries of government programs. Why should the great multitude of middle-class Americans spontaneously agree to give more of their income to the poor through significantly increased taxation? Why should they decide to give up their high standard of living for a more "risk-free" society when the life expectancy tables show that Americans are living longer than ever before? Why should they be eager to constrain the productive sectors of the economy with more environmental regulations when so many of them earn their living from this part of the economy? Even in a Communist society this would be a concern of citizens, since environmental controls reduce the resources available for economic growth.

As an intellectual, Lindblom may not share the preferences of the great mass of Americans, but that does not mean that these preferences are manipulated or contrived or that they survive simply because they are reinforced by "propaganda." It is certainly true that if a disciplined revolutionary elite took over the political and military apparatus in the United States, the society could be forcibly resocialized just as the people of mainland China were. However, no law of nature suggests that people who are free from propaganda will spontaneously choose an economic system or a distribution of income that is significantly more egalitarian than America's.

The Servility of Business

CLARENCE J. BROWN

MOST BUSINESS LEADERS are fond of speaking about Adam Smith's "morality of the marketplace" that rewards the purveyor of highest quality products at the most competitive price. It is good graduation speech material—implying that "better mousetrap" competition is the regulator that brings the maximum reward to buyer, seller, and society at large.

And so it may have been back in the day when an American President could say with little fear of political reprisal, "The business of America is business."

But times have changed. Now the business of America is government. And there is every evidence that leaders of business have accepted that as a one-way street. Business schools are even teaching courses called "Doing Business in a Regulated Environment."

The ultimate servility of business was amply demonstrated during the extended recent debate on the nation's energy policy—particularly the natural gas compromise. [*Editor's note:* This article was written in November 1978.]

As various industries began to analyze the legislation, they reacted negatively: the proposals basically would mean that fuel use decisions of the nation's major industries will be made from now on in Washington rather than by economic logic at the factory management level. They were horrified by the prospect of total

CLARENCE J. BROWN is a congressman from Ohio. He was a member of the House-Senate conference committee on the Energy Act and is ranking Republican on the Joint Economic Committee. This article was reprinted by permission from the November 29, 1978, issue of the "Wall Street Journal" (©Dow Jones & Company, 1978; all rights reserved).

federal control of natural gas pricing patterned after federal control of oil prices, which has resulted in a decline in domestic production and an increase in consumption of more expensive oil from foreign sources.

So they exercised the right the Constitution guarantees every citizen: they complained to their congressmen. They explained that the energy proposals would be adverse to the nation's interest and their own. They argued it would further reduce America's domestic energy production by tying up in red tape those independent entrepreneurs who find almost all the new gas supplies. They explained how laying all the cost of expensive gas on only industrial users (incremental pricing), instead of spreading it to all who use the gas, would be harder on some factories than others and cause massive shifting of jobs. And they suggested that a six-fold increase in the cost of gas regulation would add to the already massive cost taxpayers and consumers pay and would damage American competitiveness in foreign markets.

Like the flood of concern over other legislative flops, those lobbying efforts were having some effect. By the time the August recess began, it looked as if Congress would vote down the natural gas bill.

Breakfast With the President

But that was before the White House invited the chief executive officers of major U.S. corporations to Washington for breakfast with the President and a little straight talk about the realities of doing business in a regulated environment.

They all came. After all, the heads of the world's largest profit-making corporations don't get invited that often to break bread with the head of the world's largest not-for-profit operation.

And they heard some not-so-subtle threats. The steel industry executives were told, according to press reports, that if they didn't back off opposition to the administration's flawed energy package, the administration might not set a high priority on the problems of the steel industry when tariff negotiations were next under way with the Japanese. The CEOs of textile companies and others similarly afflicted by foreign imports got the idea about the use of "administrative judgment" in an area vital to their survival.

Several businesses which were only able to operate during the last natural gas shortage because present law gave them the right to buy emergency gas supplies above controlled prices were told that the "independent" Federal Energy Regulatory Commission might not approve such transactions for companies which had fought the President's gas legislation.

An official of the Department of Energy told an official of a medium-sized oil company that DOE hoped his company officials would not interpret vigorous pursuit of regulatory discipline of the company by the department as harassment for the company's continued opposition to the gas bill.

And so it went with the hundred and more stalwart captains of the nation's greatest companies who visited the White House — and many others who were called by phone. The message (always subtle and low-key, but unmistakable) came through to company executives whether it was received firsthand or secondhand. It was transferred from board meeting to board meeting by common directors. One of the largest corporations in the nation sent out the word to its lobbyists to desist from any activities on the energy bill. After all, it was common knowledge that the Federal Trade Commission was giving the company a careful screening.

The target of a take-over attempt by another company, committed to resisting the take-over, recognized that the attempt finally may be determined by the Securities and Exchange Commission. The company's lobbyist, who had abruptly ceased his discussion of the gas bill on Capitol Hill, explained to a curious member of Congress that his company's position on the gas bill was now a "private matter" because it would not want to risk offending the administration when its case came before the SEC.

In this day and age when public decisions touch all our lives, private viewpoints on public issues are a little like other private acts—who cares! But such privacy on public issues is not a victimless crime. If a law is going to have a significant job impact on employes, cost impact on consumers, profit impact on stockholders, or hurtful impact on our nation's ability to compete abroad, should not the business leaders be expected to advise their employes, customers, and stockholders of the situation? And don't the congressmen who represent those employes, customers, and stockholders have the right to know the impacts on the interests of their constituents who will be affected?

As a matter of fact, don't the companies that will be affected have a moral obligation to speak up on the issue?

There is little doubt that Executive Branch interference with discretionary judgments of statutorily independent agencies is improper. In some cases it is specifically a crime: tampering with Federal Communications Commission cases involving the licensing of radio and television stations, for instance.

While many discretionary decisions have been vested in the President of the United States—such as the setting of target prices in tariff matters—to simplify the process of ongoing negotiations with other nations, it was never contemplated that such powers would be used to reward or punish political loyalty or to silence opposition to a legislative agenda. Collegial agencies were specifically established to avoid such improper executive influence.

In the game of stare-down over the natural gas bill, the leaders of American free enterprise had looked into the eyes of a weak President—and blinked. And it was not an "imperial" President riding high in the polls. This capitulation by the leaders of capitalism occurred weeks before Camp David when President Carter was hovering at about the same popularity as President Nixon after the House Judiciary Committee voted for impeachment.

Regulations as Weapons

The excuse for such pusillanimity is that the fifteen-foot shelf of federal regulations passed by Congress has put a vast arsenal of weapons for punishment in any administration's hands. And the justification for doing business this way in a regulated environment is that, according to press reports, similar events occurred not only in the Senate during consideration of the natural gas bill but also in the House during consideration of the public works bill override.

Post-elective-service job opportunities were said to have been dangled before congressmen by the administration in consideration of the administration position.

Executive Branch decisions about the location of federal breeder reactor research, defense contracts, and public works projects cancellations are obvious considerations in critical votes by those who want the area they represent to be aware of their clout in Washington.

That desire for clout is no less an ambition of the political action committees of the business community. A study of their contributions shows little or no relationship to the regulatory or economic philosophy of the congressional recipients. The political dollars go to those who are in power, and the more power they have, the more money the business community delivers.

Since the natural gas debate, the President has announced a program to stop inflation by setting out "voluntary" wage and price guidelines to be enforced by the application of Executive Branch discretion. That is, industries that do not observe the wage/price advisories will find themselves with more import competition than those that do. Unions asking wage settlements above the voluntary levels may see federal projects in their industry reduced. Beyond the announced sanctions, what assurance do we have that the President will not resort to a misuse of regulatory power such as sending OSHA or EPA inspectors after a company raising its prices?

Why shouldn't the President use such weapons in the economic arena when they worked so well in the legislative arena?

Unless, of course, someone speaks up.

PART TWO

How the Market
Outwits the Planners

DAVID STOCKMAN

"RELENTLESSLY ACCUMULATING EVIDENCE suggests that human life on the planet is headed for catastrophe," Professor Charles Lindblom gravely intones in the opening paragraph of *Politics and Markets*. The harbingers of this catastrophe, in his opinion, are (1) a population growth rate that could produce a world population of 40 billion within a century and (2) a growth rate in natural-resource requirements that could lead to a thousand-fold increase over current consumption within a century. Overpopulation, resource depletion, and environmental degradation are examples of "mega-problems" that Lindblom believes can be solved only through government planning. The other writers in this volume focus on Lindblom's theory that corporate power prevents the introduction of central planning in the United States. I will examine his assertion that because we are headed for a global crisis, central planning is necessary.

The worth of simple linear extrapolation as a predictive tool was deftly illustrated by Mark Twain, who once prophesied that the Mississippi River would terminate in Minneapolis by the year 2400

DAVID STOCKMAN is the director of the Office of Management and Budget and a member of President Reagan's Cabinet. He wrote this article for the Ethics and Public Policy Center in 1978, when he was a congressman from Michigan. He has a degree in history from Michigan State University.

if its then current rate of siltation continued. Taking a worst-case approach, an analyst might project either a catastrophic crush of population or a catastrophic thousand-fold increase in industrial consumption of resources; but he would not forecast both at once, for it has long been evident that rapid industrialization is associated with a steady decline in the rate of population growth.

This association between rapid industrial growth and a decline in the rate of population growth can be seen in the record of every one of the older societies that industrialized rapidly during the nineteenth and early twentieth centuries. For those societies that have become industrial in the more recent era of modern medicine and birth control, the evidence is even more conclusive. In South Korea, for instance, between 1960 and 1977, when industrial development accelerated rapidly, the birth rate dropped from 42.4 per thousand to 24 per thousand. Moreover, the evidence accumulates that mature industrial societies eventually settle toward steady populations; this is true in most of Western Europe and seems increasingly evident in the United States as well.

Moreover, Lindblom's forecast ignores another empirically grounded rule: at least one-half of long-term industrial growth has been accounted for by an increase in the labor supply—i.e., population growth. As the populations of industrial societies stabilize in response to the social and cultural effects of affluence, the rate of industrial growth declines because improvement of productivity becomes the sole source of growth. In short, the tendency of long-term economic advance is to depress the growth rates of both population and industry. I suggest as a more realistic forecast for the next 100 years a population of, say, 15 billion and a two-hundred-fold increase in natural-resource requirements.

Prescient Planning, Wrong Results

Lindblom's failure to analyze the resource-depletion hypothesis should embarrass him. His exhaustive treatment of economic systems shows an acute awareness of the central attributes of markets: their capacity to conserve scarce economic resources, and the potent role of the price mechanism in determining the best resource mix for any production task. Why, then, does he ignore these mechanisms entirely, proposing instead a quantum leap in strategic planning? Surely not from want of historical evidence.

Consider, for example, the planner of 1880 who manages to project correctly the U.S. population and economic growth rate to 1980. Then, after laboriously calculating lumber requirements on the basis of then current figures of board feet needed per capita and per dollar of GNP, he concludes that by 1980 the planet will be stripped bare of every tree and shrub to provide material for building the houses, schools, barns, factories, sidewalks, and streets that the 1980 population will require. But once the land is denuded of vegetation, the carbon dioxide level will drastically increase, thereby sharply raising the mean global temperature; then the polar ice caps will melt, and civilization will perish in a modern version of the Great Deluge.

Fortunately, American society of 1880 did not have a place for futurist planners, nor did it have the computers that make such speculative modeling possible. The market was left to take its course: the pressure of growing demand forced up the price of lumber, causing the development of substitute building materials—steel, aluminum, cement, and plastics—derived from more abundant resources.

Then there is the prescient planner of circa 1900 who forecasts the supply, demand, and price of copper by the year 2,000. Correctly foreseeing the fantastic growth of the then embryonic telephonic communications industry, he projects the need for millions of miles of copper telephone wires and undersea cables by the close of the century. Being familiar with copper geology, he also forecasts the early depletion of the planet's high-grade copper deposits, which were then yielding copper for about $1 per pound (1978 $). Imagine his chagrin, however, if he were to appear today and find, not an acute copper shortage, but a glut in which the real price of copper is 40 per cent *below* its 1900 price.

Even the most catholic and up-to-date thinkers in 1900 could not necessarily have foreseen that the intellectual capital embodied in today's advanced copper mining and smelting technology would make it economical to mine increasingly lower-grade

copper deposits, or that the copper demand curve would fall drastically away from its geometric trend as a result of the substitution of
silicates and modern electronics-based telecommunications
technology (a communications satellite containing sixty pounds of
copper will accommodate the same volume of simultaneous trans-
atlantic messages as an undersea telephone cable requiring 2,000
tons of copper). As any given resource becomes scarce, the price
mechanisms generate resource substitutions that cause long-term
supply-and-demand curves to shift in ways unimaginable to
Lindblom's heroic planners.

Around 1910 comes the agricultural planner, petrified by the
implications of his discovery that fully 100 million of America's
400 million acres of arable cropland are devoted to the production
of fodder and roughage for draft animals, the horses and mules
used to pull heavy loads. Correctly forecasting both the rate of
agricultural output necessary to feed the 1980 U.S. population at
projected 1980 income levels and the number of draft animals
necessary to achieve this rate, he darkly announces to the nation
that by 1980 most of the arable cropland will be needed to feed the
horses and mules.

But the development of the internal combustion engine permitted the substitution of fossil-based energy for animal power,
thereby freeing 100 million acres for the production of food for
human consumption, plus vast amounts of labor for more productive employment in the industrial sector. The spectacle of
thousands of the nation's farmers parading around the White
House during the winter of 1978 in their gasoline-powered iron
horses to protest low farm prices caused by *excessive* food production was most definitely not a part of our agricultural planner's
long-range scenario.

Had the United States some decades ago incorporated the capacity for effective long-range planning that Professor Lindblom
specifies, there would doubtless have been many similar false starts
along the way. As a matter of historical record, in the 1920s the
U.S. Interior Department did begin working on shale-extraction
and coal-liquefaction technologies in anticipation of the imminent
depletion of the nation's conventional petroleum deposits. Had

Lindblom's planning authority been in place, Congress would undoubtedly have been persuaded to maintain the high war-time tax levels in order to subsidize development of a large-scale, high-cost shale-extraction and coal-liquefaction industry. But there was no central planning agency, and Treasury Secretary Andrew Mellon drastically slashed the taxes, thereby inaugurating a period of unprecedented national prosperity. The Interior Department's synthetic petroleum projects were allowed to languish, and the marketplace found Spindletop and other prodigious petroleum reserves underlying the cattle province of Texas.

A planner worth his salt in 1920 might also have forecast the depletion of high-grade iron ore deposits by the mid-1950s. But the marketplace generated new technologies that permitted a switch to far more abundant taconite reserves, even though their average iron content was less than one-fourth of that contained in traditionally mined ores.

Finally, contemplate the horror of the "solid fuels planning division" when in 1920 it finished its half-century forecast of coal production requirements and their implications. The linear extrapolation based on the 1918 coal production base of 677 million tons annually and the 1900-1918 growth rate of 5.4 per cent per annum came up black: by 1970 annual production would rise to nine billion tons, the coal labor force would number ten million, everything would be covered with coal storage yards and soot (the planners did not know about the more dangerous side-effects such as black lung, sulfur-dioxide pollution, and acid mine drainage), enormous coal transportation bottlenecks would develop, and, of course, the threat of resource exhaustion would once again loom on the horizon.

But, predictably, the relentless cost-minimizing pressures of the marketplace came to the rescue. The thermal efficiency of boilers was improved markedly; the advent of diesel engines eliminated the need for coal to power its own transportation to market; heating units fueled by natural gas, petroleum, and electricity forestalled the universal blanket of soot; coal yards were covered over with plant extensions (one reason why many steam plants cannot now convert back to coal in accordance with the dictates of current energy planners); because of mechanization and open-pit mining, coal mining required only one hundredth of the projected work force; and the frightful railroad transportation bottleneck was averted by a $75 billion nation-wide grid of underground oil and natural gas pipelines. All in all, U.S. coal production in 1970 was significantly *lower* than in 1918, not larger by a magnitude of fifteen, as the "coal planning division" might well have forecast.

Dross Into Gold — A Market Motive

The market is a powerful and well-nigh unfailing engine of resource conservation. Through the mechanism of price change it invariably shifts demand away from the scarcest resources and impels men to apply their minds to the creation of technologies that can transform dross into gold. After all, at the time of the great "whale oil shortage," petroleum was a useless nuisance that had the unfortunate habit of leaching to the surface, often where people were endeavoring to perform "useful" economic activities.

As society exhausts the supply of high-grade, low-cost, easy-to-use mineral ores and energy deposits, it proceeds toward a widening base of lower-quality deposits that must be upgraded to usable form through the application of more of man's labor, mediated by his expanding reservoir of capital and intellectual resources. This is the "grand substitution."

Most surely the recent alarm-mongering about the "energy crisis" and, in particular, about the imminent depletion of fossil fuels, one of the mega-problems that haunt Professor Lindblom, betrays a failure to comprehend this basic resource equation. At the time that the energy sky started falling in the aftermath of the 1973 OPEC embargo, for example, cumulative world production of conventional crude oil from Colonel Drake's original Titusville well to the present stood at less than 300 billion barrels. Yet the consensus in the geologic literature was that reserves of conventional petroleum that could be recovered with existing technology amounted to around 2,000 billion barrels. Thus the popularly conceived age of "petroleum scarcity" began before even 15 per cent of the resource had been exhausted.

How did this misperception arise and why does it persist? It must be attributed in very large part to the same planner's mentality that Lindblom would invest with substantial new powers to make societal decisions. The essential impulse of the planner is to pierce and dispel the veil of uncertainty that hangs over society's long-term future by extrapolating resource supply-and-demand trends, and then to impose regulations, management schemes, and other trend-altering constraints on current patterns of production and use in order to insure balance for the indefinite future.

What planners everywhere fail to recognize, however, is that *future uncertainty is an inherent corollary* of the basic impulse that propels economic life, whether under market-price systems, centralized state-directed systems, or the array of variants in between. That impulse is the universal striving of men and societies to increase wealth and living standards by getting more for less— more output or utility for less resource input. Particular economic systems and institutional arrangements frequently frustrate or dilute this cost-minimizing imperative, but they eliminate it entirely only at their ultimate peril.

The Limits on Proving Potential

The planning mentality fails to comprehend four patterns of natural-resource development and use. First, there are inherent limits on the rate at which potential resources are translated into proven reserves. The seismic and geophysical testing, exploratory drilling, log analysis, and other activities involved in proving petroleum reserves, for example, are costly, even in the prodigious fields of the Middle East. Since time erodes the current value of assets producible in the distant future, the market simply refuses to indulge in the orgy of current expenditures required to prove the entire potential resource base for any given mineral, or even some substantial fraction of it. The interest rate, the cost of reserve acquisition, and the expected future price of the resource cause the market to impose definite limits on the proven resource inventory it will carry. Despite the planner's yearnings to the contrary, society has better things to do with its current income than stock the next century's pantry shelves—with possibly obsolete goods.

Take the case of the worldwide crude oil potential. At the time of the 1973 embargo it was true that more than half of the 2,000-billion-barrel resource base represented "speculative resources" that were not part of the proven reserve inventory. But this condition primarily reflected inventory saturation. In 1973, the worldwide ratio of proven reserves to production already exceeded 30 to 1. In some of the new petroleum provinces the rapid buildup of excessive reserve levels in the 1960s had nearly extinguished further exploratory activity. In Saudi Arabia, for example, the 1977 reserves-to-production ratio stood at 50 to 1. Not surprisingly, during 1977 only eight exploratory wells were drilled in the entire country—despite ample geologic evidence of substantial additional reserves.

Evidence accumulating since 1973 confirms the view that the uncertainty over the crude oil resource base reflects economics-based inventory limits rather than a low probability of physical availability. Between 1973 and 1977, worldwide crude oil production totaled 80 billion barrels, while additions to reserves exceeded 100 billion barrels. In the period since the petroleum-exhaustion hypothesis gained currency, the rate of reserve acquisition has not slowed down at all, as it would have done if the estimates of ultimately recoverable reserves had been drastically excessive. Indeed, with the recent huge increase in the estimated size of Mexican reserves, it appears that the rate of reserve acquisition is accelerating, and that the geological resource estimates of the early 1970s are probably conservative. The highly regarded 1975 resource-base estimates of J. D. Moody, for example, place ultimately recoverable reserves for the entire Western Hemisphere south of the Rio Grande at 166 billion barrels; yet a few years later Mexico alone estimated a potential in the 200-300 billion range.

Reserves at the Frontiers

A second misperception that nourishes the planner's alarm about imminent petroleum exhaustion stems from the fact that most of the undiscovered potential reserve lies in frontier areas—

the Arctic regions, Siberia, hazardous offshore waters, tropical areas, and other parts of the less developed world. The fact that these new petroleum frontiers lie at the frontiers of the civilized industrial world apparently causes great apprehension for the planner.

The geologic sciences hold that the hydrocarbon creation process was a planet-wide phenomenon. Through such processes as fossilization, sedimentation, and temperature and pressure changes, a network of petroleum deposits was created. These deposits vary in size, quality, and accessibility. They were laid down according to a precise internal logic—one that bears no relation to the logic that dictated the distribution of modern industrial oil-consuming populations.

The original petroleum provinces—western Appalachia, the Ukrainian fields, and various small fields in Europe—were located close to their markets, the industrial centers. But as modern pipelines and ocean tankers steadily reduced the costs of transportation, oil fields were developed at ever greater distances from market: the Texas Gulf, western Canada, Venezuela, Soviet Siberia, and eventually the Persian Gulf and North Africa. Similarly, as lower-cost onshore deposits were used up, the search shifted to high-cost offshore areas; as shallower reservoirs gave out, drilling went deeper; as high-gravity sweet crudes became scarcer, lower-gravity sour crudes were exploited; and as naturally pressured reservoirs were used up, artificial recovery techniques were applied to less desirable deposits.

The significant point, however, is that throughout the first century of the petroleum era, the real price of crude oil steadily declined. This meant that the cost-reducing technology necessary to recover what had previously been uneconomical deposits developed faster than the market demand for additional production. The proportion of the resource base that had been either produced or inventoried before the 1973 embargo, therefore, reflects the complex workings of the least-cost imperative. The crude oil that had been extracted or inventoried was that whose cost—for exploration, production, transportation, and refining—was lowest.

This also explains why more than a trillion barrels of conventional crude oil remained undiscovered in 1973: since ample production inventories could be maintained at the prevailing price, there was little reason to develop technologies that could bring the more costly frontier regions into production. At the pre-embargo price of roughly $2 per barrel, production in Alaska's North Slope would have been uneconomical because the transportation cost to the U.S. markets is approximately three times that price; similarly, the high-paraffin Chinese oil would not have been marketable at that price because of the substantial extra refining cost it required; and even most of the North Sea fields would have been marginal propositions at the prevailing $2 price.

Since cartelization of Persian Gulf reserves in 1973 had the effect of quadrupling the real price of oil, vast portions of the undiscovered resource base were suddenly rendered economic. Because OPEC has shown it intends to uphold the price of world oil by withholding production, the global marketplace has been unleashed to produce oil from previously marginal reserves so long as costs-to-market can be held below the new price. Drilling rigs are now moving into undiscovered portions of the petroleum resource base not primarily because new geologic information has reduced uncertainty as to their existence but because new price signals have made them economically accessible. In the absence of undue interference by governments and planners, the global marketplace will have no trouble maintaining adequate inventory acquisition rates for many decades.

The Potent Process of Substitution

The third defect in the planning mentality is the failure to grasp the potent process of resource substitution. Industrial economies do not require crude oil from conventional deposits; they merely need liquid hydrocarbon raw materials that can be refined into a variety of products. The global potential to supply these is simply mind-boggling. No major breakthroughs in science, engineering, or technology would be required, and the price of such supplies would be perhaps not more than double the current crude oil price.

The most plentiful of these lower-grade reserves that can be upgraded into suitable liquid and gaseous fuels is coal. Recoverable reserves are estimated at the equivalent of 12 trillion barrels. The reason why the gasification and liquefaction plants necessary to process coal into usable fuels have not been built is not that the technology is lacking; these plants would employ standard industry engineering, chemistry, temperatures, and materials. The reason is purely economic: conventional crude oil is still cheaper to find and produce. The same economic logic explains why deposits of heavy oils, tar sands, and shale reserves, all available in huge quantities in the Western Hemisphere alone, have not been fully explored, mined, and converted into usable fuel.

Finally, even the two-trillion-barrel conventional oil resource base has substantial potential for expansion. It represents an estimated four to six trillion barrels of existing oil, the greater part of which is deemed not recoverable at current prices using available technology. But recent investigations of the potential for new technology to push beyond the current 25 to 40 per cent recovery rates suggest the likelihood of hundreds of billions of additional barrels recoverable within the limits of an affordable price range and achievable technology.

Overall, the planet's accessible natural hydrocarbon reserves readily exceed 20 trillion barrels. This is the equivalent of *five centuries of consumption* at current rates. The figure would be even greater should recovery of the abundant geo-pressurized gas reserves prove to be economic. The scientific or technological advance required is of a far lower order than that developed for the moon landing or for current fusion-power experiments.

Thus, barring an uncharacteristic and suicidal decision by industrial societies to forgo even modest technological advances, there is simply no prospect that fossil fuels will be depleted within any relevant period of time.

The Growth Rate of Demand

The final type of uncertainty that makes the planner apprehensive is the projected increase in demand for energy resources. The planner may object to the assertion that our planet has five centuries' worth of nature-made fossil reserves on the grounds that this figure represents current consumption rates rather than geometric growth over time.

But very few things compound at constant rates over long periods, as our hypothetical "solid fuels planning division" of 1920 learned. The striking evidence for this proposition as it applies to energy-consumption growth rates is already available. Prior to 1973, world energy consumption was growing at 5 per cent annually, a compounding rate that yields some pretty staggering supply requirements even a few decades into the future. This projection was based on the supposition that economic growth in the countries that are the major consumers of world energy would create a corresponding growth in energy use.

But this supposition was invalidated by the dramatic energy price change of October 1973. In the countries of the Organization for Economic Cooperation and Development (OECD—some two dozen countries, mostly in Western Europe but including the United States, Japan, Australia, and New Zealand), the real GNP increased by 9 per cent between 1973 and 1977; energy demand during that period increased only 1.3 per cent, a drastic reduction from the previous trend. Indeed, by 1977 the "savings" from efficiency improvements and non-fuel substitution was equivalent to 5.5 million barrels per day—the entire daily production of Iran.

The more important point, however, is that this dramatic reduction in energy input relative to economic output did not represent "conservation" in the moralistic sense of doing without or reducing final utility. Instead, it reflects the use of more insulation and therefore less heating fuel; better refinery plumbing and engineering and therefore less fuel consumption per barrel of refined output; and lighter transportation equipment and therefore lower fuel consumption per vehicle mile. In thousands of ways, the market pursues the least costly way of achieving the work that society wants done.

In the final analysis, the planner has no faith in the capacity of the marketplace to generate technologies that will, say, transform tar sands into kerosene, waste heat into productive fuel, or shredded newspaper into an efficient component of home heating systems.

As a result, he drastically underestimates the natural-resource potential available to society for the creation of wealth, and he counsels a course of hoarding, austerity, and economic stagnation. Yet precisely such enforced scarcity tends to dull the incentives and block the market mechanisms that lead to the creation of wealth and technological advance.

Air and Water in the Marketplace

Professor Lindblom's third mega-problem—environmental degradation—is really another aspect of the general problem of resource scarcity. What does "pollution" mean if not the using up of finite resources of clean air and water? Given man's fixed biological needs for air and water, the substitution process that prevails in the market is somewhat restricted in scope; however, nothing prevents it from reducing the industrial consumption of air and water.

Because the common law came to view air and water as indivisible resources and therefore "free goods," it is not surprising that the untrammeled marketplace moved toward using them as dumping grounds for unwanted byproducts; this was the cheapest method of disposal. Nor is it surprising that the solution to this practice is to put a price on emissions so that water and air enter the marketplace calculation at a cost that reflects their scarcity.

Over the past decade, every industrial society has been doing just that, albeit sometimes through clumsy and inefficient pricing mechanisms such as plant discharge permits and regulatory standards rather than the preferred means of emission fees and taxes. The results have been dramatic in many areas. The average 1965 automobile, for example, spewed out 90 grams of carbon monoxide per mile; the 1978 model emitted just 15 grams per mile. The 1977 *Report of the Council on Environmental Quality* showed substantial improvement in the level of each of the five regulated air pollutants and similar results for water quality. In short, once the unaccounted-for costs to society resulting from lack of defined property rights in air, water, and other environmental resources are recognized and appropriate prices are imposed on these resources, there is every reason to believe that the so-called pollution problem can be handled through the joint efforts of marketplace and polyarchy.

Why then does Professor Lindblom foresee global asphyxiation or poisoning? One superficial mathematical reason is not convincing. It is the argument that if, over time, world output rises by many orders of magnitude, even stringent reductions in *unit emissions* (such as hydrocarbons per vehicle mile or sulfur dioxide per ton of coal burned) will not prevent the *total volume of pollution* from rising to levels intolerable for human health.

Once again we are confronted with an implausible linear projection and a failure to appreciate the dynamics of price. The fact is that most pollution forms (particulates, sulfur dioxide, nitrogen oxide, carbon monoxide) stem from combustion and other chemical transformations of fossil energy or from the reduction and purification of virgin ores. Yet the prospect of rising real prices over time for all three critical variables—environmental resources, fossil fuels, and virgin ores—implies some substantial shifts in their growth curves. As ore grades decline, energy costs rise, and pollution controls become more stringent (hence more costly per unit of output), there is a decrease in the price advantage of finished materials derived from virgin ores over finished materials extracted from recycled resources. And as more recycled resources are included in the volume of materials used to produce any given level of GNP, the volume of pollutants is likely to drop sharply. For instance, the pollution load per ton of recycled aluminum is only 8 per cent of the pollution load per ton of aluminum derived from bauxite.

Similarly, the anticipated rise in real prices for both fossil fuels and environmental resources can be expected to generate strong economic pressure toward closed-cycle industrial technologies in which both energy requirements and pollution loads per unit of final output decline dramatically. Industry transforms materials by a long series of "huff and puff" cycles. As materials move from the raw state to final form, each "huff"—heating to high temperatures—requires prodigious amounts of energy, and each "puff"—cooling—spews forth pollutants and contaminants.

Every time a "huff and puff" cycle is removed by new technology, both energy requirements and pollution loads decline.

Take for example the coking process: coal is heated to above 2,000 degrees Fahrenheit to produce the coke needed for fueling the blast furnace; then the coke is removed from the oven and transported down the line to the blast furnace. Currently, the problem posed by the extreme oxidizing potential of hot coke when exposed to air is handled by a quenching cycle, and the results are polluted water, polluted air, and a huge dissipation of heat energy. A vacuum conveyance to transport hot coke directly from the oven to the blast furnace would eliminate this quenching cycle, with its large energy loss and pollution load.

To devise such a technology would be difficult and costly but not impossible. Rising prices for energy and environmental resources will prompt the paper, chemical, and basic-metals industries to replace the open-cycle technologies developed during the years when resources were cheap with closed-cycle technologies that conserve air, water, and heat. And so the amount of pollution emitted is not necessarily going to increase as output increases.

Why Pessimism Persists

These things should be evident enough even to the generalist. But the fear that man will eventually so befoul his nest as to threaten extinction of the race persists. Why?

Let me tentatively suggest a reason for the extreme pessimism about the pollution problem shared by observers such as Professor Lindblom. Thus far most of the decisions on pollution-control standards have not been made in the Congress, simply because these matters are too technical and complex for the average legislator. The rules have been devised in agencies in which three groups have been dominant: mission-oriented bureaucrats, highly specialized health and medical professionals, and professional environmental activists. Each of these groups has an interest in pressing for pollution-control standards that are excessively stringent when viewed in relation to economists' conventional notions of optimal social welfare.

The power of regulatory bureaucrats, external assessments of their performance, and the amount of political risk to which they are subject all turn on how effectively they pursue the single task assigned to them. The motive of minimizing political risk is an especially important source of decision bias among the environmental bureaucrats. If the rate of economic growth declines because unnecessarily burdensome costs have been placed on environmental resources, the regulation writers at the Environmental Protection Agency are unlikely to receive a major share of the blame, simply because there are many theories of what causes economies to prosper or languish. But if a large number of smog-related deaths occur, the political blame will be rather precisely placed. Hence the bias toward a rather generous "margin of error," as the term is used in the Clean Air Act.

The professional and ideological interests of the other two groups that are dominant in the regulatory agencies—the specialized health and medical professionals and the professional environmental activists—generate the same single-value bias. In short, what should be a task of making the best trade-off among many values falls mainly to single-value maximizers who do not give adequate attention to other values. As a result, air and water quality is likely to continue to fall short of the federal standards—not because the air and water are too dirty and we are headed for an environmental catastrophe but because the standards are too stringent. Environmental resources are already being husbanded carefully enough to insure that no extraordinary threat to society's long-run future will arise.

The Obstacle to Planning

Lindblom's analysis of the problem of influence in the polyarchy may state the case upside down. The problem may be, not that the polyarchy is too weak in coping with the various institutionalized forces of the marketplace, or that it is paralyzed by the veto of the business elite, but that its tendency and capacity to act are too great.

If, as the previous essays in this volume suggest, it is not the influence of business in the United States that prevents the introduction of central planning and any serious effort to radically redistribute the nation's wealth and income, what *is* the obstacle? I have an alternative explanation to suggest.

The U.S. version of polyarchy tolerates a great deal of costly folly: it wastes national resources subsidizing peanut growers and barge lines; it frequently bails out undeserving corporations, industries, and unions, such as Lockheed, the steel industry, and the building trades; it often overuses the Federal Reserve printing presses in a vain effort to stimulate more production by issuing more money—only to widen swings in the business cycle and generate alternating bouts of inflation and unemployment, and sometimes both at once; and it provides more public goods and services than the people really want to pay for (as evidenced by the recent tax revolt) because producer groups and other special-interest constituencies (such as social workers, educators, research scientists, nutritionists, homebuilders, environmentalists) can mobilize to influence the decision-making process.

But these "excesses" have their limits. As Senator McGovern learned in 1972, the American public will not permit an arbitrary effort by government to alter radically the distribution of the general wealth and income of the nation. This is because the public intuitively knows that despite the frequent dissatisfaction of some groups with particular market outcomes, the general rewards of the marketplace are essential to maintain the level of wealth and standard of living that the market generates. The public will apparently tolerate the use of government taxing and subsidizing powers in limited instances involving the limited extension of indulgences and penalties. But it resolutely forswears the ultimate application of these powers—taxing half the population down to the mean and subsidizing the other half up—which is the essence of the kind of redistribution Professor Lindblom seeks.

In the same measure, it permits all kinds of limited tinkering with the market system that might vaguely smack of planning, such as demand-management policies, health planning, urban planning, and agricultural market stabilization. But in every instance during this century in which wartime exigencies have installed authentic central planners in positions of real power, the public's response has been swift and unmistakable: before the ink on the peace treaty was dry, it elected a Republican Congress to insure that those chaps were issued their walking papers.

Lindblom appears to have more in common with his former critics on the left than with the plethora of participants in the polyarchy he so ably described in earlier works. He fundamentally disapproves of the way the American people have chosen to order and manage their affairs and sympathizes with the century-old illusion of the Left that a new man, a new social order, and a new world are possible if only right-thinking intellectuals gain or seize power. It's a pity, however, that in order to tell us this he had to write a whole book, invent imaginary catastrophes, concoct implausible power elites and strategic vetoes, and mar what was otherwise a fairly serviceable model of how democratic societies operate.